WHEN GOD CALLS

DAWN THOMAS

When God Calls

Copyright © 2019 by Dawn Thomas

ISBN (Print Edition): 978-1-54398-433-0
ISBN (eBook Edition): 978-1-54398-434-7

ADDITIONAL ACKNOWLEDGEMENTS

When God Calls gives biblical answers to many of life's toughest questions: What happens when we die? How can I cope with the loss of a loved one? Will I see them again? This is far from a dry textbook, however. Mrs. Thomas wrote an engaging, conversational book that weaves biblical teaching around the story of the death of her son. I highly recommend When God Calls for all who are struggling with the loss of a loved one. I gave it to my friend whose wife has terminal cancer and it blessed them both. You will learn. You will cry. You won't put it down and you will celebrate the salvation that only Jesus offers all those who give their lives to Him.

Jon Benzinger – Lead Pastor
Redeemer Bible Church

Loss and grief are a reality of living in a fallen world. A couple of the difficulties in understanding the grieving process is that people do not grieve in the same way nor in the same period of time. When God Calls will help the reader wherever they are in the process. The beauty of When God Calls is that it is biblically centered and gospel rich! As Dawn Thomas shares her life and the loss of her precious son, Ryan, she will bring the reader to our true hope, our true comfort, a sovereign God that is working out every detail of life.

Tom Angstead - Pastor/Elder Grace Bible Church
Director of Biblical Counseling of the East Valley

The subject of death is often met with empty and hopeless platitudes in our culture, leaving people with unanswered questions about this world, and the God who created it. Thankfully, Dawn Thomas has taken this issue head-on by not only intimately sharing her own experiences in dealing with an unexpected and tragic loss of a son, but she also thoughtfully handles and shares what the Bible has to say about this topic. I encourage you to not only read When God Calls for yourself, but to buy one for your pastor as well; it would be a gift for him.

Dale Thackrah, MA
Sr. Executive Pastor - Redeemer Bible Church

For Ryan

All Glory Be to God!

TABLE OF CONTENTS

Introduction

A Time for Everything

For everything there is a season,
and a time for every matter under heaven:
a time to be born, and a time to die;
a time to plant, and a time to pluck up what is planted;
a time to kill, and a time to heal;
a time to break down, and a time to build up;
a time to weep, and a time to laugh;
a time to mourn, and a time to dance;
a time to cast away stones, and a time to gather stones together;
a time to embrace, and a time to refrain from embracing;
a time to seek, and a time to lose;
a time to keep, and a time to cast away;
a time to tear, and a time to sew;
a time to keep silence, and a time to speak;
a time to love, and a time to hate;
a time for war, and a time for peace.

The God-Given Task

What gain has the worker from his toil? I have seen the business that God has given to the children of man to be busy with. **He has made everything beautiful in its time. Also, he has put eternity into man's heart, yet so that he cannot find out what**

God has done from the beginning to the end. *I perceived that there is nothing better for them than to be joyful and to do good as long as they live; also that everyone should eat and drink and take pleasure in all his toil—this is God's gift to man. I perceived that whatever God does endures forever; nothing can be added to it, nor anything taken from it. God has done it, so that people fear before him. That which is, already has been; that which is to be, already has been; and God seeks what has been driven away.* (Ecclesiastes 3:1-15)

As he was writing these words, King Solomon understood that everything under the sun—past, present and future—is created and controlled by a loving, generous, merciful, and sovereign God; and, most importantly, that all He does endures forever. *No one* can add to or delete anything God has done from eternity past to eternity future.

I want to focus on verse 11: *He has put eternity into man's heart.* What does that mean? All human beings born into this world will die a physical death. What no human being can know is when. We have no say regarding when we will be born or to whom we will be born; and it is God's choice to determine when we are going to die. When the Giver of life and death calls us, our time is up. When our predetermined days on earth are complete, we don't have the luxury of bargaining; we cannot rewind the clock; and there are no second chances. We are all living on borrowed time.

What we can do is prepare ourselves and our loved ones to die without fear. We can face death with an assurance that provides peace, healing, and hope in an ever-dying world.

When I initially began writing this book, it was my goal to address parents who had lost a child. But God had another plan in mind—a wider audience. This book is for anyone who has lost a loved one—whether child, parent, brother, sister, grandparent, aunt, uncle, or cousin—and who is experiencing pain, suffering, and a hurt that doesn't dissipate. Perhaps you or someone you know is in the midst of *the valley of the shadow of death.* (Psalm 23:4) So, while these words come from a mother who has experienced the loss of a child, they are applicable to all who have experienced, or who are currently experiencing, the loss of a loved one.

If you are a believer, a disciple of Jesus Christ, and have gone through the pain and suffering of losing a loved one, my prayer is that the words of this book will bring you continued peace, assurance, healing, and hope. I also want to encourage you to teach others that this life is but a mist of the sea, a vapor in the wind. What is most important is eternal life and where your soul will be when God calls.

If you are not a believer and are struggling with the pain and suffering of losing a loved one, my prayer is that by the time you have read the last page, you will have a better understanding of death through the eyes of peace, assurance, and hope; and that you will be able to answer life's greatest question: **Where will I spend eternity should God choose to take my soul today?**

CHAPTER 1

A Mother's Cry ~ Part 1

I can't think of many mothers who don't brag about their children in some way. While I'm no exception, the focus of this book far outweighs me talking about Ryan. I will, however, give you a synopsis of the character of God's creation I've known as my son, as seen through the eyes of his mother.

From the time he was born, Ryan was full of life. He smiled almost all the time. He was an adventurer and risk-taker. He loved and played sports (especially football), was a big brother, and a genuine friend to many. He worked hard. He played hard and loved life. He was kind and patient (especially with his little brothers). And he acquired a love of hunting from his Dad. Okay, that was the good stuff.

Like all of us, Ryan didn't always make the wisest choices. To give an example: At the age of five, toward the end of kindergarten, he and a buddy walked off the school grounds and headed down a major road. When school personnel caught up with them, Ryan told them he and his buddy wanted to see the Grand Canyon, and so off they went. Okay . . . really? Two 5-year-olds actually thought they could make it to the Grand Canyon from Phoenix! When asked if he knew where the Grand Canyon was, Ryan said he didn't. He just knew it was in Arizona and figured they would find a way to get there.

Another time, when he was in high school, Ryan and a buddy arranged (they told their parents) to go skiing for the weekend; only later did we find out they went to Rocky Point, Mexico. There were a few other "adventures," but I won't bore you with the details since the point I want to make is this—because of sin, we all have made unwise choices that have consequences. I do want to add a side note: Almost every time Ryan got caught (and he got caught 99% of the time), he owned it; he never lied, which was refreshing. I used to tell him over and over that he would always get caught. One, because God sees it all; and two, because God loves him and will admonish him one way or the other. I honestly believe that's why he always told the truth; he had a genuine fear of the Lord. I don't mean fear in that he was afraid of the Lord. By fear, I mean he loved and respected God.

To sum up—in his short twenty-one years on earth, Ryan lived life.

Two Months Prior

As a mother you spend your life teaching—teaching your children to walk, talk, learn, grow, behave, listen, have fun, and become the man or woman they are meant to be. Ryan was the first-born of three boys. Always on the go, he loved life, smiled all the time, and I can't remember too many times when he was in a bad mood. Unless he was in trouble. He was the adventurous one. By the age of twenty-one he'd tried just about everything in life. He loved the outdoors. He loved to hunt. He worked hard. He studied hard. He played hard. He loved hard. Ryan just loved life. Except for a few bad choices, Ryan was what every mother wants her son to be. Most importantly, Ryan loved God and had a deep respect for His Maker.

He was just beginning his third year of college as a communications major. It was a hot, humid, mid-August Arizona day. He called me and said, "Mom, I need a place to live. My roommate situation has dissipated." He had just turned twenty-one and, at the time, what was going through my head was, *Oh, no . . . college, late nights, working, and twenty-one. I'll have zero control.*

Well, here I was thinking about such trivial matters, while God in His gracious, loving providence was working it out to give me one-on-one time with my son before calling him home. But, even more precious to me was what God did just two weeks prior to His call.

It's during times like these that we must stop and realize God's amazing loving kindness and grace. For those of you who know God's assurance, peace, and hope, think about what He did for you prior to losing your precious loved one.

CHAPTER 2

Physical Death, Spiritual Death and the Soul

There are a myriad of ways in which physical death comes our way. Here are just a few—

- Disease
- Natural disaster
- By the hands of another (murder)
- Self-inflicted (suicide)
- Accident (land, water, air, train)
- Famine, beasts
- Natural causes
- Drugs, alcohol
- Wars

Death brings a sharp, painful sting to all of us. It cuts right through the heart and bleeds into the depths of our being with no mercy. In a matter of seconds, it can bring absolute despair and thrust you into a place of helplessness, leaving you vulnerable and exposed and thinking you cannot go on. I'd often thought that nothing could hurt more than a parent losing a child, but that is a selfish perspective. To some level, death hurts all of us. The aftermath of the loss of a loved one has destroyed marriages, broken up families, ended friendships, caused depression, and can catapult us into superficial ways of coping. For many, broken hearts and broken spirits with no sense of hope yields to a life devoid of peace and hope. *Without hope human beings will fade into depths of despair and cease to live.*

Death's grand deception is that it is the end, that once someone dies there is no life. Nothing could be further from the truth. In this chapter, I want to touch on why we die—physically and spiritually—and show you how physical death brings eternal life. Once you understand how this works, you'll discover how to have peace, understanding, and hope.

Physical Death -The Reason We All Will Die

In Acts 10:34 the Apostle Peter tells us that God shows no partiality toward any person, in any nation, at any time. I mention this passage to say that how you die or when you die has nothing to do with whether you are a believer. We live in a sin-cursed world and death is going to come to us all. To get the full grasp of why this is, we must turn to Genesis 3. In this passage God clearly instructed Adam and Eve that they would die if they ate from the *ONE* tree forbidden to them.

> *And the Lord God planted a garden in Eden, in the east, and there he put the man whom he had formed. And out of the ground the Lord God made to spring up every tree that is pleasant to the sight and good for food. The tree of life was in the midst of the garden, and the tree of the knowledge of good and evil.* Jumping to verse fifteen, *The Lord God took the man and put him in the garden of Eden to work it and keep it. And the Lord God commanded the man, saying, "You may surely eat of every tree of the garden, but of the tree of the knowledge of good and evil you shall not eat, for in the day that you eat of it you shall surely die.* (Gen 3:8-9; 15-17)

What did God mean, "You shall surely die?" I'm not sure Adam and Eve understood, because they had been created perfectly and knew no sin. Looking at the last verse of Genesis 1, God saw everything He made and it was *very good*. So, Adam and Eve "knew perfection, no shame (as they were naked and did not know it) with no knowledge of evil before the fall, even nakedness was shameless and innocent."[1] Not only did they have no knowledge of evil, they never even had an evil thought, they knew no pain, no calamities, no struggles, no diseases, and no death. But at the moment of their disobedience to God, *the eyes of both were opened, and they knew they were naked.*

Here, my friends, is where sin entered the world. Here is where physical and spiritual death began and, most importantly, eternal damnation of the soul. Because we are the offspring of Adam and Eve, every human being born into this world from the time of their fall is born into sin. The Apostle Paul clearly points this out: *Therefore, just as sin came into the world through one man, and death through sin, and so death spread to all men because all sinned.* (Romans 5:12)

Spiritual Death

Because of sin, not only do we suffer an earthly physical death, but of greater gravity and eternal consequence, we suffer spiritual death. What does that mean? Remember, God created Adam and Eve perfectly; they were formed in His image and knew no sin, only goodness. They were not sovereign; they were not omniscient (all-knowing), omnipresent (present everywhere), or omnipotent (all powerful) as God is. Even so, man was created to live eternally. So, when Adam and Eve sinned, there was immediate separation (spiritual death) from God. *Spiritual death is the soul being separated from God.*

---

1   MacArthur Study Bible Notes (ESV).

What is Sin?

So, what is sin? We know that disobedience was Adam and Eve's downfall. But have you ever wondered what constitutes sin? Unfortunately, in our culture, and in many previous generations, sins are no longer called sin, but "mistakes." Perhaps this is done to minimize guilt. But I ask you: Have you ever at some point in your life lied, cheated, stolen, had fits of rage or anger, been envious, jealous, disobeyed, lusted, or sexually impure? (To name a few.) I venture to guess the answer is, "Yes," for all of us. We are imperfect. So, let's take a look at what sin is.

In a sermon he preached to his congregation, "What is Sin?" Dr. John MacArthur defines sin: "Sin is any personal lack of conformity to the moral character of God, or the law of God. Sin is a disposition of the heart; it is a bent. It thinks evil, it speaks evil, it acts evil, and it omits good. You sin when you do, when you say, when you think, or when you don't do, say, think what God commands you to." The Bible identifies sin in 1 John 3:4: *Everyone who makes a practice of sinning also practices lawlessness; sin is lawlessness.* Whose law? God's law. God has revealed His law in Scripture. Sin and God are incompatible.

You see, sin begins in the heart and mind. Jesus in Matthew 15:18-19 tells us where sin begins when He states: *"what comes out of the mouth proceeds from the heart....for out of the heart come evil thoughts.."* So, no matter how you present yourself outwardly, God has center stage and a front row seat to everything that goes on in your heart and mind.

Sin is the reason physical and spiritual death comes to us all. Matthew Henry, in his commentary on Genesis 3:16-19, sums up life and death since the fall of Adam: "Human life is exposed to many miseries and calamities, which very much embitter the poor remains of its pleasures and delights. Some never eat with pleasure, through sickness or melancholy; all, even the best, have cause to eat with sorrow for sin; and all, even the happiest in this world, have some allays to their joy: troops of diseases, disasters, and deaths, in various shapes, entered the world with sin, and still ravage it."[2]

Now that we have a greater understanding why all human beings born into this world die physically and are spiritually dead upon arrival, the remaining focus of this book will be on the answer to life's greatest question; the most important question every human being should ask themselves. But first, we need to lay the foundation.

What Is the Soul?

What is the soul? What is its significance? What makes human beings different from other created creatures; such as, the birds of the air, the fish of the sea, and the beasts of the field? How many times have you heard at a funeral, or from a friend or family member who may be grieving, that the deceased person's soul is in a better place? What does that mean?

Let's go back to Genesis 2:7, when God created man. *And the LORD God formed man of the dust of the ground and breathed into his nostrils the breath of life; and man became a living soul.* (King James Version) To answer the question, "What is the soul?" we need to examine a few Scripture verses to get a full understanding. In Genesis 1:26-27, God said: *Let us make man in our image, after our likeness. And let them have <u>dominion over</u> the fish of the sea and over the birds of the heavens and over the livestock and over all the earth and over every creeping thing that creeps on the earth. So, <u>God created man</u> in his own image, in the image of God he created him; male and female he created them.*

What does it mean to be created in God's image? The word *image* in this context means man's unique relationship to God. God created man a living being capable of expressing His communicable (moral) attributes; such as

---

2   Matthew Henry, *Genesis 3,* Matthew Henry's Commentary of the Whole Bible – Six Volumes (Hendrickson Publishers, 2014 pg.).

love, kindness, goodness, mercy, patience, wisdom, justice, and forgiveness. John MacArthur explains: "In his rational life, (man) was like God in that he could reason and had intellect, will and emotion. In the moral sense, he was like God because he was good and sinless."[3] Additionally, to be created in God's image means that He gave man the ability to have and enjoy relationships; such as, sharing emotions and sharing your heart and soul. No other creature has this ability, only man. God gave man a personality, rationality, emotions, intellect, reasoning, awareness, and spirituality.

While God breathed life into animals, fish, and birds (Genesis 7:21), the difference between the breath He breathed into animals and the breath He breathed into man is that when God breathed into the nostrils of Adam, Adam became a living soul. The breath of life that was breathed into man was the <u>image of God</u>.

Only man was created in God's image. As John Wesley notes in his commentary on Genesis 2: "And the soul takes its rise from the breath of heaven. It came immediately from God; he gave it to be put into the body. The body would be a worthless, useless carcass, if the soul did not animate it."[4] And in 1 Corinthians 15:45: *The first man, Adam, was made a living soul.* The quality of our life is our living soul. Thus, Job 33:4: *The Spirit of God has made me, and the breath of the Almighty gives me life.*

You may ask, "Why is this important?" It's important because God created us—our souls— for eternity, just as He is eternal. So, although the physical body (carcass) dies, our souls belong to God. We were created immortal. There is no other passage in the Bible that states this more clearly than Ezekiel 18:4: *Behold, all souls are mine; the soul of the father as well as the soul of the son is mine: the soul who sins shall die.* Solomon, the Preacher, states it well: *And the dust returns to the earth as it was, and the spirit (soul) returns to God who gave it.* (Ecclesiastes12:7)

---

3   MacArthur Bible Study Notes.
4   John Wesley, *Wesley's Explanatory Notes*, n.d.

Jesus also spoke of the soul when he corrected the false teaching of the Sadducees who didn't believe in the resurrection of the dead: *And as for the resurrection of the dead, have you not read what was said to you by God: "I am the God of Abraham, and the God of Isaac, and the God of Jacob?" He is not God of the dead, but of the living.* (Matthew 22:31-32)

So, now that you understand why death occurs both physically and spiritually, the only remaining question is: Do you know where you will go when you die and why you will go there? There are only two places to go, heaven or hell. And think about this . . . it will be for eternity. Forever and ever!

CHAPTER 3

Eternal Life

A Mother's Cry ~ Part 2

Two Weeks Prior To The Accident – God's Mercy #1

About two weeks prior to God calling Ryan home, I had begun making dinner and Ryan was sitting on the couch watching TV. There was a report on the news about someone who had died. As we were talking about the sadness of the death, Ryan suddenly said to me, "Mom, I am not afraid to die. I know God is in control of life and death and I know where I am going when I die. I know I will be with God." My initial thought was, *WOW! That was profound. And perhaps a bit out of character for a son who, at times, lived his life on the edge.* But as he looked me in the eyes with the utmost sincerity, I responded: "Ryan, to know YOU have that peace and assurance in God for yourself, gives me no greater peace as a parent." It was an amazing grace-filled, all-encompassing love moment that God graciously gave me assuring me of my son's salvation.

What is Eternal Life?

We all can agree that death comes to us all. Some of us die in the womb, some die at birth, some in adolescent years, young adult years, mid-life years, and some not until we are very old. But we all die. And for many of us, death's sting—whether anticipated or sudden—catches us unprepared; unprepared mentally, physically, emotionally, and spiritually. Why?

The old saying, "time heals all wounds," is nothing but a farce. Time cannot heal anything, much less a broken heart or spirit. What time (our mind) does is put a band-aid on the wound, giving it a superficial sense of healing. We also know that time does not stand still. Life goes on. And we are forced to move forward. But as life moves on, does time bring peace, hope, and assurance? Whenever we face death, there is not a human being that does not consciously wonder, "Is this it? You die and return to dust? Or could it be that there really is life after death? Is there truly a heaven and hell?" We intrinsically want to know that physical death is not the end. Why?

The answer to this question depends on whether you believe your soul is immortal. Historically, most cultures and societies—whatever their religious beliefs are—believe in some form of life after death and the immortality of the soul. Many, if not most of us, have a sense of longing to see our loved ones again, especially when death becomes a stark reality.

You may ask, "Why is it, deep in a man's heart, he wants to believe in eternity?" Because God has set eternity in every human heart, as Ecclesiastes 3:14 states. We feel the lure of eternity because our Creator placed it there. God created us to live forever because He is eternal. He created us in His image. Through the breath of life we have eternal, immortal souls. He placed our souls into a physical body to live forever with Him.

John Wesley's notes on Genesis 2:7 explains: "The Lord God, the great fountain of being and power, formed man. Of the other creatures it is said, they were created and made; but of man, that he was formed, which notes a gradual process in the work with great accuracy and exactness." Wesley goes on to state: ". . . the body of man is curiously wrought. And the soul takes its rise from the breath of heaven. It came immediately from God; he gave it to be put into the body." Referring to Ecclesiastes 12:7, he emphasizes that the dust returns to the earth as it was and the spirit returns to God who gave it. Then: "'Tis by it that man is a living soul, that is, a living man. The body would be a worthless, useless carcass, if the soul did not animate it."[5]

From the Old Testament to the New Testament, the Bible—God's revealed Word—speaks of eternal life.

> *For I know that my Redeemer lives, and at the last he will stand upon the earth. And after my skin has been thus destroyed, yet in my flesh I shall see God, whom I shall see for myself, and my eyes shall behold, and not another. My heart faints within me!* (Job 19:25-27)

> *The Lord knows the days of the blameless, and their heritage will remain forever.* (Psalm 37:18)

> *He asked life of you; you gave it to him, length of days forever and ever.* (Psalm 21:4)

> *And many of those who sleep in the dust of the earth shall awake, some to everlasting life, and some to shame and everlasting contempt.* (Daniel 12:2)

> *Truly, truly, I say to you, whoever hears my word and believes him who sent me has eternal life. He does not come into judgment, but has passed from death to life.* (John 5:24)

> *For this is the will of my Father, that everyone who looks on the Son and believes in him should have eternal life, and I will raise him up on the last day.* (John 6:40)

> *Jesus said to her, "I am the resurrection and the life. Whoever believes in me, though he die, yet shall he live, and everyone who lives and believes in me shall never die."* (John 11:25-26)

---

5   John Wesley, *Wesley's Explanatory Notes*, n.d.

Let not your hearts be troubled. Believe in God; believe also in me. In my Father's house are many rooms. If it were not so, would I have told you that I go to prepare a place for you? And if I go and prepare a place for you, I will come again and will take you to myself, that where I am you may be also. (John 14:1-3)

For the wages of sin is death, but the free gift of God is eternal life in Christ Jesus our Lord. (Romans 6:23)

Who but God could reveal and share with us eternity? His Word tells us how He made us, why He made us, and that our souls will live for eternity. But what does eternality mean? The answer is revealed in a later chapter. What we need to grasp now is the finality of eternity and our coming fate. We are all going to die physically, and our material body will return to dust. But our souls (and soon to come our resurrected bodies) will live for eternity, and there are only two places to go after we physically die, heaven or hell. So now that the groundwork has been laid that we were created for eternity, it's important for us to get a better understanding of the sovereignty of God.

CHAPTER 4

Understanding the Sovereignty of God

A Father's Grief—Part 1

Ryan and his dad had a typical father-son relationship. Ryan had so many of his Dad's characteristics—friendly, outgoing, never knew a stranger, loved to talk, loved and played sports, and loved to hunt. They bonded over their shared interests and in the last couple years of Ryan's life, their relationship moved beyond father-son, developing to a deep friendship.

Kevin was driving out of town on a pre-planned trip and was about four hours away, when he learned about Ryan's death. His initial reaction was disbelief and shock. How long that drive back to town must have been for him; and how alone he must have felt. I remember him telling me that Ryan wanted to go scouting with him that day, but because of the trip he was unable to go. He told me if he had just gone scouting, Ryan would still be here. *No,* I said to myself, *not God's plan.*

This chapter is perhaps the most important chapter of this book, the heart of the book. How well you grasp it will depend on how you view God. My prayer is that as you read, you will be able to grasp the width and depth of the sovereignty of God, and the amazing freedom, comfort, and hope his sovereignty provides for those in the depths of despair. Understanding God's sovereignty will answer your whys—

- Why do some die in a car accident while others survive the same accident?
- Why are some children murdered at the hands of a school shooter while others survive?
- Why do drug addicts survive lengthy addictions while others take the drug one time and die?
- Why does one cancer patient die within days or months of a diagnosis while others survive years?
- Why do some people have a heart-attack or stroke and die instantly while others survive?
- Why do some people survive a natural disaster while others perish?
- Why are there many attempted suicide survivors, while others are successful?
- Why do some soldiers survive war while others are killed in battle?
- Why do some babies die in the womb while others live to be 90 and100-years-old?

It is not uncommon to question the "unfairness" of death. Neither is it uncommon to try to come up with some rational reason why people die unexpectedly. For instance, we think perhaps the person who died in a car accident wasn't wearing a seatbelt; the person who died taking drugs for the first time was allergic to the drug; the cancer simply wasn't caught "in time"; or the sudden heart-attack or stroke victim had a pre-existing condition. Those who perished in a natural disaster were simply living in the wrong place at the wrong time; or the attempted suicide survivor failed to take necessary measures to ensure death. The war survivors just happened to be in the right place, at the right time. As for babies who don't survive the womb, maybe the mother wasn't in good health or the baby wasn't strong enough to survive.

But what about the unexplainable? A car accident so massive that all should have perished; or the drug addict who has overdosed multiple times, yet still survives. What about the athlete who is in remarkable physical shape, yet suddenly dies on their morning run? The war survivor who is in the same place at the same time as their fellow soldiers, yet the bullets or IED did not take their life? The construction worker who survives after a rod pierces his skull, missing a major vein within millimeters, yet doctors were able to remove it without inflicting major damage? The massive heart-attack patient who was given a one-percent chance of survival, yet survives? The tsunami that wipes out the village or town causing multiple deaths, yet some survive? What about those who survive an attempted murder or mass murder? What about those who make every assurance to ensure their suicide, yet fail?

We could go on and on attempting to understand the whys behind death, maybe even call the unexplainable a miracle. I call it—the explained and unexplained—God's sovereign providence over the hows, the whens, the wheres, and the whys of all humanity's physical death. For a believer, knowing how a loved one dies, when a loved one dies, where a loved one dies, and why a loved one dies is irrelevant; all of it is under God's control. This frees me from thinking or believing there was anything I could have done. We are not in control of such things and it is foolish to think otherwise. Friends, our loved ones die simply because that's when God calls them home.

What Does Sovereignty Mean?

In Merriam-Webster's Dictionary the word sovereign means, "above or superior to all others, chief, supreme; supreme in power rank and authority, royalty, independent of all others."[6] Easton's Bible Dictionary defines God's sovereignty as His "absolute right to do all things according to his own good

---

6   Merriam-Webster Dictionary

pleasure."[7] Synonyms for sovereignty are: dominion, rule, power, control and authority. The following verses attest to this definition:

> All the inhabitants of the earth are accounted as nothing, and he does according to his will among the host of heaven and among the inhabitants of the earth; and none can stay his hand or say to him, "What have you done?" (Daniel 4:35)

> I am the Lord, and there is no other, besides me there is no God; I equip you, though you do not know me, that people may know, from the rising of the sun and from the west, that there is none besides me; I am the Lord, and there is no other. I form light and create darkness; I make well-being and create calamity; I am the Lord, who does all these things. I made the earth and created man on it; it was my hands that stretched out the heavens, and I commanded all their host. (Isaiah 45:5-7,12)

> I perceived that whatever God does endures forever; nothing can be added to it, nor anything taken from it. God has done it, so that people fear before him. (Ecclesiastes 3:14)

The Westminster Confession of Faith states: "God, from all eternity, did, by the most wise and holy counsel of His own will, freely, and unchangeably ordain whatever comes to pass."[8] A. W. Pink says, "The sovereignty of the God of the Bible is 'absolute, irresistible and infinite.' God does as he pleases, when he pleases and with whom he pleases and all in accordance to the counsel of his will."[9]

When we speak of the sovereignty of God, we assert that He is the Almighty who is in complete power and control of heaven and earth. God is omniscient (all knowing), omnipotent (all powerful), and omnipresent

---

7   Easton's Bible Dictionary, n.d.
8   Westminster Confession of Faith, *Ch. III - Of God's Eternal Decree*, I.
9   AW Pink, *The Sovereignty of God*, 1999.

(always present). Because He is the creator of heaven and earth, His sovereignty establishes the right to govern the universe as he pleases and for His glory. "Sovereignty characterizes the whole being of God. He is sovereign in all His attributes. He is sovereign in the exercise of his power. His power is exercised as He wills, when He wills, and where He wills."[10]

I love the absoluteness of Dr. Steven Lawson's description on the sovereignty of God from his teaching series, *The Attributes of God*. "It is God's supreme authority and his right to exercise his sovereignty over His creation. He actively reigns over the heavens and earth and hell itself. It is his supreme right.

The Lord HAS ESTABLISHED HIS THRONE IN THE HEAVENS, AND HIS KINGDOM RULES OVER ALL. (Psalm 103:19)

Say among the nations, "The Lord REIGNS!" (Psalm 96:10)

Yes, the world is established; it shall never be moved; He will judge the peoples with equity. Men do not reign, circumstances do not reign, good luck is not reigning, bad luck is not reigning, blind fate is not reigning, there are no accidents, no random occurrences. There is only one who is actively reigning, and it is God! Every moment of every day, God is reigning. He reigns over nations, He reigns over nature, He reigns over events, He reigns over circumstances. He reigns over good people; He reigns over evil people. He reigns over human minds and even over human wills. Proverbs 21:1: *The king's heart is a stream of water in the hand of the Lord; HE TURNS IT WHEREVER HE WILL.* God is determined to execute His will. Proverbs 16:9: *Man plans his ways; God directs his steps.*

God overrules our lives. There is only Plan A, never a Plan B. So even though we may second guess ourselves and say, "If I had only done this or that," it doesn't matter, as God always works His Plan A for our lives. God

---

10   ibid

guarantees that His sovereign will, will come to pass. God declared how things are going to happen and turn out in eternity past before anything, God is the architect of the master plan for the entire universe."[11]

The Ways God Is Sovereign

Now that you have been given a good dose of the definition and description of the sovereignty of God, I want to take a look at some of the ways He is sovereign, using scriptures that attest to His everlasting sovereignty over all and at all times. Note, these scriptures just scratch the surface of of all that could have been selected.

God's Sovereignty in Creation (Heaven, Earth, Land, Sea, Man, Animals, Vegetation)

Whatever the Lord pleases, he does, in heaven and on earth, in the seas and all deeps. (Psalm 135:6)

The Lord has made everything for its purpose, even the wicked for the day of trouble. (Proverbs16:4)

Worthy are you, our Lord and God, to receive glory and honor and power, for you created all things, and by your will they existed and were created. (Revelation 4:11)

Many are the plans in the mind of a man, but it is the purpose of the Lord that will stand. (Proverbs 19:21)

Remember the former things of old; for I am God, and there is no other; I am God, and there is none like me, declaring the end

---

11   Steven Lawson, *The Attributes of God - Teaching Series*, 2014.

from the beginning and from ancient times things not yet done, saying, "My counsel shall stand, and I will accomplish all my purpose." (Isaiah 46:9-10)

God's Sovereignty Over Nations and People

Should anyone ever doubt the outcome of elected officials or rulers of nations, these scriptures should bring comfort.

For kingship belongs to the Lord, and he rules over the nations. (Psalm 22:28)

God reigns over the nations; God sits on his holy throne. (Psalm 47:8)

The Lord brings the counsel of the nations to nothing; he frustrates the plans of the peoples. The counsel of the Lord stands forever, the plans of his heart to all generations. (Psalm 33:10-11)

Man plans his ways, but God directs his steps. (Proverbs 16:9)

The king's heart is a stream of water in the hand of the Lord; he turns it wherever he will. (Proverbs 21:1)

The Lord has established his throne in the heavens, and his kingdom rules over all. (Psalm 103:19)

The plans of the heart belong to man, but the answer of the tongue is from the Lord. (Proverbs 16:1)

He changes times and seasons; he removes kings and sets up kings; he gives wisdom to the wise and knowledge to those who have understanding. (Daniel 2:21)

For by him all things were created, in heaven and on earth, visible and invisible, whether thrones or dominions or rulers or authorities—all things were created through him and for him. And he is before all things, and in him all things hold together. (Colossians 1:16-17)

God's Sovereignty Over Trials and Suffering

In him we have obtained an inheritance, having been predestined according to the purpose of him who works all things according to the counsel of his will. (Ephesians 1:11)

I know that you can do all things, and that no purpose of yours can be thwarted. (Job 42:2)

For the Lord of hosts has purposed, and who will annul it? His hand is stretched out, and who will turn it back? (Isaiah 14:27)

As for you, you meant evil against me, but God meant it for good, to bring it about that many people should be kept alive, as they are today. (Genesis 50:20)

Then the Lord said to him, "Who has made man's mouth? Who makes him mute, or deaf, or seeing, or blind? Is it not I, the Lord?" (Exodus 4:11)

In Matthew 10:26-31, Jesus is teaching His disciples about persecution and what life may bring being those who follow Him. It is in this context that He tells His disciples not to fear those who can kill the body, **but to fear Him who kills both the body and soul**. He then goes on to tell them how precious they are to God: *Are not two sparrows sold for a penny? And not one of them will fall to the ground apart from your Father. But even the* *hairs of your head are all numbered. Fear not, therefore; you are of more value than many sparrows.*

What is so powerful in Jesus' teaching to the disciples is His affirmation "that God providentially controls the timing and circumstances of such insignificant events as the death of a sparrow. Even the number of hairs on our heads is controlled by His sovereign will. In other words, divine providence governs even the smallest details and mundane matters."[12]

God's Sovereignty Over Life and Death

Since his days are determined, and the number of his months is with you, and you have appointed his limits that he cannot pass. (Job 14:5)

For you formed my inward parts; you knitted me together in my mother's womb. I praise you, for I am fearfully and wonderfully made. Wonderful are your works; my soul knows it very well. My frame was not hidden from you, when I was being made in secret, intricately woven in the depths of the earth. Your eyes saw my unformed substance; in your book were written, every one of them, the days that were formed for me, when as yet there was none of them. (Psalm 139:13-16)

See now that I, even I, am he, and there is no god beside me; I kill and I make alive; I wound and I heal; and there is none that can deliver out of my hand. (Deuteronomy 32:39)

The LORD KILLS AND BRINGS TO LIFE; HE BRINGS DOWN TO SHEOL AND RAISES UP. (1 Samuel 2:6)

---

12   MacArthur Study Bible Notes

And he made from one man every nation of mankind to live on
all the face of the earth, having determined allotted periods and
the boundaries of their dwelling place. (Acts 17:26)

So, as you can see, everything and everybody (all of creation) is under the sovereign control of God. "God in his perfect knowledge, his perfect power, his perfect holiness and expressing his perfect love has ordained everything."[13]

God sovereignly predestined and ordained from the foundations of the world the life and death of every human being. Each of us has a certain number of days, months, and years to live that were established and set before creation. **So, whether your loved one passed from a disease, at the hands of another, by an accident, natural disaster, suicide, heart-attack, or drug-overdose, those were the allotted days God chose for them to be on earth. The means of how one dies is only the vehicle by which death eventually comes to us all.** The folly of man is to think that we somehow have the ability to control our own destiny, including death. According to Proverbs 16:9: *Man plans his ways, but God directs his steps.*

You might be saying, "That's not fair! Are you telling me that my child, spouse, or loved who was murdered, or died of a disease, or was killed in an accident—even at the hands of another—could not have been prevented?" Yes, that is exactly what I am telling you. You, your child, spouse, or any loved one has predetermined days here on earth ordained by God (Job 14:5). That is why we must live our lives each day prepared to die. That is why we must focus on eternity, not on things of this earth, because when your soul has been called, there are no second chances. That is the lesson from the book of Ecclesiastes: Everything is vanity, because it will all vanish like vapor. As Jesus said in Mark 8:36: *For what does it profit a man, to gain the whole world, and forfeit his soul?*

---

13   John MacArthur, *Why Does Evil Dominate the World?* Mar. 4, 2007.

We put everything into our children, our spouses, our jobs, our friends, our family, our communities; and we put so little, if anything, into the assurance of eternal life. None of us knows when our souls will be required of us. Our focus must be God-centered; our foundation must be God-driven. We must learn about the God of the Bible. We must teach our children about the God of the Bible. Most assuredly, if God called you, your child, your spouse, or any loved one this very minute, you must know the answer to life's greatest question: Where am I going to be spending eternity? Or, as the lawyer (scribe) asked Jesus: What do I do to inherit eternal life?

One last note before we move on to our next chapter. We must always remember that children are a gift from God (Psalm 127:3). Every life born is a blessing and a reward, not only in times of joy, but also in times of sadness and sorrow. So often we are possessive of our children as if we owned them. We do not. As Ezekiel 18:4 taught me: *Behold, all souls are mine.* Every soul is owned by God. The most precious gift we could ever give our children is to lay a foundation for a life well-lived on earth with a focus on eternity. *Train up a child in the way he should go; even when he is old he will not depart from it.* (Proverbs 22:6)

CHAPTER 5

Two Places to Spend Eternity

A Mother's Cry—Part 3

God's Call, October 4, 2008

I t was a beautiful Saturday morning. In addition to going to school full time, Ryan was working two jobs, with the second job mainly on the weekends. He had gotten home extremely late (early morning hours) from his job, so I was surprised to see him up early this Saturday morning, as I knew he was tired and that he was working again that evening. However, because of his love for doing anything outdoors, he and some friends had planned one last water-skiing rendezvous, knowing the cooler weather was just around the corner and it would be the last time for the season. He got up, put on his swim trunks, told me he was going skiing and would be back by 3:00 or 4:00 p.m. to get ready for work. My last words to him were, "I want your room cleaned up by tomorrow and I love you." Sounds just like a mom, doesn't it? To this day, I scold myself for once again picking on the trivial things in life.

I went about my day, watched some football, and ran errands. I remember trying to call him to see if he had made it home yet, but received no answer. Arriving home sometime between 5:00 and 6:00 p.m., I realized Ryan had not been home. I just assumed he'd called his work, thinking the lake, friends, and a long day had probably gotten the better of him.

Your life can change suddenly, in a nanosecond, as mine was about to.

The knock.

It surprised me. It was around 7:00 p.m. There was an officer at the door with another woman whom I later learned was grief counselor. When I opened the door the officer said, "Are you the mother of Ryan Thomas?" To be honest with you, my first thought was, *What has he done now?* I replied that I was Ryan's mother and the officer requested to come in to speak with me.

At this point, my heart started to race. I guided them up the stairs to the kitchen. My youngest son, Jacob, was with me, and a friend. I asked Jake to leave the room, but he wanted to stay. The officer confirmed that Ryan had gone to the lake with friends and had gone skiing. He then told me the boat had docked, waiting in line to unload, when Ryan jumped into the water. He never came up. The authorities had spent the last several hours searching for him, but had not yet found him.

I screamed. I heard my son scream. I said this was not possible. Ryan's a great swimmer. I fell to my knees and crawled to the bathroom, thinking I was going to be sick. I just kept saying this can't be happening, this isn't true, you've got the wrong information. Complete and utter denial. The pain at that moment is a pain I will never forget; it is so heavy and piercing that it feels like your heart is literally breaking.

After a few minutes, I knew I had to call his Dad. This was the second hardest thing I have ever done, and frankly didn't do a very good job. I was crying so hard, I was unable to get out what needed to be said. The officer took the phone and explained what had happened. The next most difficult calls were to my son, Joshua, who had recently completed bootcamp and was stationed in Hawaii preparing for his first deployment to Afghanistan, and to my parents who were living in Arkansas.

I would like to devote these next chapters to biblical descriptions of heaven and hell. What is shared and discussed will only scratch the surface. These passages were chosen for the purposes of this book. There are many commentaries, books, and articles on heaven and hell that are more complete treatments of the subject. I encourage you to locate them and read them.

Much of what is to be explored in this chapter is taken directly from the Bible, as the Bible is the authoritative source regarding heaven, hell, death, and eternity. In addition to scripture, quotes and excerpts have been selected from sermons by Jonathan Edwards—including, "The Torments of Hell Are Exceedingly Great" and "The Justice of God in the Damnation of Sinners"— as well as passages from other notable theologians, teachers, and pastors.

While many may claim they do not believe in heaven or hell, the Bible says otherwise, as God has placed eternity in every man's heart: *He has made everything beautiful in its time. Also, he has put eternity into man's heart, yet so that he cannot find out what God has done from the beginning to the end.* (Ecclesiastes 3:11) God—in His infinite wisdom, grace, and mercy—gave us this knowledge so that, when physical death occurs, we may know that this life is not the end. In America (according to a Gallup Poll taken in May and June 2016), roughly 77% of the people polled said they believe in heaven; 64% said they believe in hell; approximately 85% said they believe in God; while 77-80% said they believe in Jesus. This being the case, it is only fitting that we take a look at what the Bible says about heaven and hell.

Considering that nothing is more certain than death, it is essential that we honestly assess our current state. Most people live every day as though tomorrow will come; we plan for this, we plan for that. We spend every waking moment busying ourselves with the day's events, taking for granted that the next minute, hour, and day will come. We make daily plans. We make plans for our future. We even make appropriate plans (like wills and life insurance policies) to benefit our loved ones in the event of our death. But what about an eternal life insurance policy? Think about it. Our thoughts are entrenched in this world with little or no consideration regarding life to come. What we *don't* do each day is live as though we are prepared for death. I don't mean being prepared financially or having a will. What I mean to say is: If you were to die today, do you know where you would go—heaven or hell? A simple one-word answer isn't enough. We must also ask ourselves: How do I know? What assurance do I have?

When attending a funeral, how many of us think about our own eternity? How many of us wonder what the person who died is experiencing? I venture to say we don't put much thought into eternity at all, for ourselves and much less for the one who died. Why? Because we are so caught up in our own emotions. Take a moment and think about persons you know who have died. They are living in either heaven or hell, their eternal home. Think about it. Let it settle into your thoughts. Is my son, daughter, spouse, parent, grandparent, aunt, uncle, cousin, friend, co-worker or other loved one spending eternity in heaven or hell? Then ask yourself, If God should require my soul today, where would I spend eternity? How do I know? What assurance do I have?

James, the half-brother of Jesus, put it into perspective when he wrote:

> Come now, you who say, "Today or tomorrow we will go into such and such a town and spend a year there and trade and make a profit"— yet you do not know what tomorrow will bring. What is your life? For you are a mist that appears for a little time and then vanishes. Instead you ought to say, "If the Lord wills, we will live and do this or that." As it is, you boast in your arrogance. All such boasting is evil. So whoever knows the right thing to do and fails to do it, for him it is sin. (James 4:13-17)

Erwin Lutzer, Pastor of Moody Church in Chicago, wrote in his book, *One Minute After You Die*:

One minute after you slip behind the parted curtain you will either be enjoying a personal welcome from Christ or catching your first glimpse of gloom as you have never known it. Either way, your future will be irrevocably fixed and eternally unchangeable...and so while relatives and friends plan your funeral—deciding on a casket, a burial plot, and who the pallbearers will be—you will be more alive than you have ever been. You will either see God and His throne surrounded by His angels and redeemed humanity, or you will feel an indescribable weight of guilt and abandonment. There is no destination midway between these two extremes; just gladness and gloom. Nor, will it be possible to transfer from one region to another, no matter how endless the ages, no matter how heartfelt the cries, no matter how intense the suffering, your travel plans are limited to your present abode. Those who find themselves in the lower, gloomy regions shall never enter the gates that lead to endless light and ecstasy. They will discover that the beautiful words spoken in their eulogy bear no resemblance to the reality that now confronts them.[14]

How many times have you heard at a funeral that so and so is "in a better place"? I ask: How do you know? Your response might be, "Well, he was a good person," or, "Look at all they did for mankind. Look at their philanthropy; how they gave to the poor, helped so many in need. They had good morals and a good character." Some may add, "They were a religious person." But I tell you, this is exactly the opposite of what God says. So many people believe they are "good" people and their "good deeds" will pave their way into heaven. They delude themselves into believing that God will overlook their small sins; that God would never send them to hell. We live in a society that has all but erased the word sin; and in so doing, many fool themselves

---

14   Erwin W. Lutzer, *One Minute After You Die*, 2015.

into believing they are good persons and deserve to be in heaven. Here is what God says about our goodness:

None is righteous, no, not one; no one understands; no one seeks for God. All have turned aside; together they have become worthless; no one does good, not even one. (Romans 3:10-12)

All we like sheep have gone astray; we have turned—every one—to his own way; and the LORD HAS LAID ON HIM THE INIQUITY OF US ALL. (Isaiah 53:6)

For all have sinned and fall short of the glory of God. (Romans 3:23)

Because God is holy, righteous, and just, He must punish sin. In his sermon, "Torments," Jonathan Edwards states:

Rebellion against God's authority and contempt of his majesty, which every sin contains, is an infinite evil, because it has the infinite aggravation of being against an infinitely excellent and glorious majesty and most absolute authority. A sin against a more excellent being is doubtless greater than against a less excellent; and therefore, sins against one infinite in majesty, authority and excellency must be infinite in aggravation, and so deserves not finite, but an infinite punishment, which can be only by its being infinite in duration. And then one sin deserves that the punishment should be to that degree of intenseness as to be the destruction of the creature, because every sin is an act of hostility, and 'tis fit that God's enemies should be destroyed. [15]

Have you ever lied? Have you ever cheated or stolen anything? Has anger ever gotten the best of you? Remember, any sin—no matter how great or how small—is a sin against God and, by definition, a sin is any offense committed

---

15   Jonathan Edwards, *"The Torments of Hell Are Exceedingly Great."* n.d.

against God. King David clearly understood this in Psalm 51:4: *Against you, you only, have I sinned and done what is evil in your sight, so that you may be justified in your words and blameless in your judgment."* Benjamin Franklin once said, "But in this world nothing can be said to be certain, except **death** and **taxes**." Well, here is another certainty: In this world nothing is more certain than death, eternity, and judgment for us all!

Notice that all this talk about sinning against God is what those who are left behind go through. What about the souls of those who have died? What are they going through? Because truly, the soul is all that matters. The soul that has departed this earthly life is now *living* for eternity in either heaven or hell—their permanent home.

CHAPTER 6

Eternity in Hell

Did you know that there are more scripture passages about hell and judgment in the Bible attributed to Jesus than anyone else? Why? 1) His purpose was to warn us of what was to come for those who did not believe. Throughout the Word of God—from Genesis to Revelation—God warns us about our choices and their consequences. It's known as the "if. . . then" principle. Because He is a God of grace, mercy and justice, there will ALWAYS be warnings before judgment. 2) Because it is Jesus who will be our judge. He will be the one to send those who refuse to believe in Him to hell.

> *For as the Father raises the dead and gives them life, so also the Son gives life to whom he will. For the Father judges no one, but has given all judgment to the Son, that all may honor the Son, just as they honor the Father. Whoever does not honor the Son does not honor the Father who sent him. Truly, truly, I say to you, whoever hears my word and believes him who sent me has eternal life. He does not come into judgment, but has passed from death to life.* (John 5:21-24)

In his teachings, using images and symbols, Jesus describes hell as a real place—such as fire, darkness, and pit—as a warning for all who do not believe in Him. For example, darkness symbolizes God's curse. Fire (lake of fire) represents separation from God's love and mercy, retribution for evil deeds, and everlasting punishment. When Jesus talks of those cast into outer darkness and "gnashing of teeth" in Matthew 25:30, this portrays their escalating anger with God as their punishment increases. This is similar to how the people reacted as they stoned Stephen in Acts.

Hell is a real place and is controlled and kept by a sovereign God. He is the jailer and holds the keys There is no way out. Why? Because God is a just God. He is not only a God of grace and mercy, but He is a God of justice. He will rightly judge and punish all *unbelieving* sinners eternally for their sins. There are no second chances and there is no more mercy.

In Dr. MacArthur's sermon, "A Testimony of One Surprised to Be In Hell, Part 1," he gave a dire description of hell:

> What if everything in your life was as bad as it could be? Take everything bad that has ever happened in your life, roll it all into one experience, and make it permanent. All the pain, all the disappointment, all the failure, all the hatred, all the bitterness, all the fear, all the anxiety; and experience that to the full, and then add this: There's no hope. It cannot, it will not ever get better. That knowledge would compound and exacerbate your suffering exponentially, incalculably. If you were in the severest torture and the most profound and relentless torment in all the realms of human faculty, physical and mental and spiritual and emotional, and you were suffering in all those realms at the same time and knew there would never be one moment of relief, nothing will ever change, forever, the suffering would be inexpressible. I just described hell. It is the place of the most profound suffering, compounded infinitely by the realization that it lasts forever, and nothing will ever change.[16]

Sounds downright frightening! Well, here's more, as we take a look at what the God-inspired biblical authors say about hell and eternal punishment.

---

16 John MacArthur, *A Testimony of One Surprised to Be in Hell, Part 1*, Apr. 23, 2006.

The prophets of the Old Testament speak of God's judgment of sinners. It is often referred to as, "The Day of the Lord."

> *Behold, the day of the* Lord *COMES, CRUEL, WITH WRATH AND FIERCE ANGER, TO MAKE THE LAND A DESOLATION AND TO DESTROY ITS SINNERS FROM IT.* (Isaiah13:9)

> *The* Lord *UTTERS HIS VOICE BEFORE HIS ARMY, FOR HIS CAMP IS EXCEEDINGLY GREAT; HE WHO EXECUTES HIS WORD IS POWERFUL. FOR THE DAY OF THE* Lord *IS GREAT AND VERY AWESOME; WHO CAN ENDURE IT?* (Joel 2:11)

> *For the day of the* Lord *IS NEAR UPON ALL THE NATIONS. AS YOU HAVE DONE, IT SHALL BE DONE TO YOU; YOUR DEEDS SHALL RETURN ON YOUR OWN HEAD.* (Obadiah 15)

> *For behold, the day is coming, burning like an oven, when all the arrogant and all evildoers will be stubble. The day that is coming shall set them ablaze, says the* Lord *OF HOSTS, SO THAT IT WILL LEAVE THEM NEITHER ROOT NOR BRANCH. But for you who fear my name, the sun of righteousness shall rise with healing in its wings. You shall go out leaping like calves from the stall. And you shall tread down the wicked, for they will be ashes under the soles of your feet, on the day when I act, says the* Lord *OF HOSTS.* (Malachi 4:1-3)

Jonathan Edwards in another sermon entitled, "Death and Judgment," gave his congregation crucial insight into the critical matters of life and death.

> In this world, sometimes, wicked men are great kings, and deal very hardly and cruelly with good men, and put 'em to death; and therefore, there must be another world where good men shall be happy and wicked men miserable.

In another world, God will call 'em to an account of what they have done here in this world; how they have improved their time, and whether they have kept his commandments or no. he will hold them to an account that have heard the gospel preached; he will ask whether or no they have repented of their sins and have in their hearts accepted of Jesus Christ as their Savior.

And then all wicked men, and they that would not repent of their sins and come to Christ, will have their mouths stopped and will have nothing to say.[17]

In the afterlife, God will balance the scales of justice. We must seek God now as our Savior, because when we die, He will become our judge. On that day of judgment, *every unbelieving sinner will be judged for every thought, motive, word and deed and it will be replayed and displayed for all to see* (Rev. 20:12). Think about the worst things you have ever done in your life. Now think about the "insignificant" sins, the ones you think didn't hurt anybody. All will be righteously judged by God who has kept meticulous records (written in the books to what they had done). Whatever the degree of punishment, it will fit the offense exactly. For those who put their faith and trust in Jesus alone will receive **mercy**; but for those who knew of Jesus and rejected him, they will receive **justice**.

The following verses are from the very words of Christ himself:

> *You have heard that it was said to those of old, "You shall not murder; and whoever murders will be liable to judgment." But I say to you that everyone who is angry with his brother will be liable to judgment; whoever insults his brother will be liable to the council; and whoever says, "You fool!" will be liable to the hell of fire.* (Matthew 5:21)

---

17   Strachan and Allen, *Jonathan Edwards on Heaven and Hell*, 2010.

And do not fear those who kill the body but cannot kill the soul. Rather fear him who can destroy both soul and body in hell. (Matthew 10:28)

I tell you, on the day of judgment people will give account for every careless word they speak, for by your words you will be justified, and by your words you will be condemned. (Matthew 12:36)

The Son of Man will send his angels, and they will gather out of his kingdom all causes of sin and all law-breakers, and throw them into the fiery furnace. In that place there will be weeping and gnashing of teeth. (Matthew 3:41-42)

In this passage of scripture, Jesus speaks on the Final Judgment:

When the Son of Man comes in his glory, and all the angels with him, then he will sit on his glorious throne. Before him will be gathered all the nations, and he will separate people one from another as a shepherd separates the sheep from the goats. And he will place the sheep on his right, but the goats on the left. Then the King will say to those on his right, "Come, you who are blessed by my Father, inherit the kingdom prepared for you from the foundation of the world. For I was hungry and you gave me food, I was thirsty and you gave me drink, I was a stranger and you welcomed me, I was naked and you clothed me, I was sick and you visited me, I was in prison and you came to me." Then the righteous will answer him, saying, "Lord, when did we see you hungry and feed you, or thirsty and give you drink? And when did we see you a stranger and welcome you, or naked and clothe you? And when did we see you sick or in prison and visit you?" And the King will answer them, "Truly, I say to you, as you did it to one of the least of these my brothers, you did it to me."

Then he will say to those on his left, "Depart from me, you cursed, into the eternal fire prepared for the devil and his angels. For

I was hungry and you gave me no food, I was thirsty and you gave me no drink, I was a stranger and you did not welcome me, naked and you did not clothe me, sick and in prison and you did not visit me." Then they also will answer, saying, "Lord, when did we see you hungry or thirsty or a stranger or naked or sick or in prison, and did not minister to you?" Then he will answer them, saying, "Truly, I say to you, as you did not do it to one of the least of these, you did not do it to me." And these will go away into eternal punishment, but the righteous into eternal life. (Matthew 25:31-46)

Eternal Punishment

What does eternal punishment look like? The Bible teaches it will be unrelenting torment, abandonment (separation from God), and it will be eternal—forever and ever. Other than God revealing to us what hell and eternal punishment will be for those who reject his gracious offer of salvation, Jesus gives us an inside peek by way of his parable of the Rich Man and Lazarus as told in Luke 16:19-31:

There was a rich man who was clothed in purple and fine linen and who feasted sumptuously every day. And at his gate was laid a poor man named Lazarus, covered with sores, who desired to be fed with what fell from the rich man's table. Moreover, even the dogs came and licked his sores. The poor man died and was carried by the angels to Abraham's side. The rich man also died and was buried, and in Hades, being in torment, he lifted up his eyes and saw Abraham far off and Lazarus at his side. And he called out, "Father Abraham, have mercy on me, and send Lazarus to dip the end of his finger in water and cool my tongue, for I am in anguish in this flame." But Abraham said, "Child, remember that you in your lifetime received your good things, and Lazarus in like manner bad things; but now he is comforted here, and you are in anguish. And besides all this, between us and you a great chasm has been fixed, in order that those who would pass from here to you may not be able, and none may cross from there to us." And he said, "Then I beg you, father, to send him to my father's house— for I have five brothers—so that he may warn them, lest they also come into this place of torment." But Abraham said, "They have Moses and the Prophets; let them hear them." And he said, "No, father Abraham, but if someone goes to them from the dead, they will repent." He said to him, "If they do not hear Moses and the Prophets, neither will they be convinced if someone should rise from the dead."

What is Jesus saying here? First, let me state there are fantastic commentaries and sermon messages on this passage that are worth your study. For our purposes, in this passage Jesus is not saying that rich people are going to be tormented in hell for being rich, neither are poor people going to be in heaven because they are poor. The Bible is clear that our economic status has nothing to do with our eternal destiny. In the days when Jesus told this parable, the Pharisees believed the richer you were, the more blessed you were by God; and if you were poor, the more cursed you were by God. In this parable, Jesus describes the exact opposite of what was a popular belief.

I have bulleted the key points of what Jesus is telling us:

- He tells us that hell is a place and heaven is a place, and upon the moment of death, both souls in the narrative are very much alive!
- He describes the person in hell as suffering, "for I am in anguish in this flame". . . "this place of torment."
- He tells us there is a chasm between hell and heaven and no one can enter or leave either place upon entering; their placement is fixed.
- Lastly, when he says, "they have Moses and the Prophets; let them hear them," Jesus makes it clear that God's Word (Scripture) leads us to repentance; and those who choose not to hear or listen to the

revealed Word of God, will also reject what is in plain sight—the Savior Jesus.

As we have seen, Jesus himself spoke of hell and eternal punishment more than any anyone else in the Bible. In addition to His teaching, the major prophets—Isaiah, Ezekiel, and Daniel—also spoke of the torments of hell:

And they shall go out and look on the dead bodies of the men who have rebelled against me. For their worm shall not die, their fire shall not be quenched, and they shall be an abhorrence to all flesh. (Isaiah 66:24)

Behold, all souls are mine; the soul of the father as well as the soul of the son is mine: the soul who sins shall die. vs. 20: The soul who sins shall die. The son shall not suffer for the iniquity of the father, nor the father suffer for the iniquity of the son. The righteousness of the righteous shall be upon himself, and the wickedness of the wicked shall be upon himself. (Ezkiel18:4)

And many of those who sleep in the dust of the earth shall awake, some to everlasting life, and some to shame and everlasting contempt. (Daniel 12:2)

In an excerpt from Jonathan Edwards' sermon, "The Torments of Hell Are Exceedingly Great," the preacher uses Jesus' parable, to describe God's wrath toward the ungodly:

The punishment that is threatened to be inflicted on ungodly men is the wrath of God. God has often said that he will pour out his wrath upon the wicked. The wicked, they treasure up wrath; they are vessels of wrath, and they shall drink of the cup of God's wrath that is poured out without mixture. Revelation 4:10, "The same shall drink of the wine of the wrath of God, which is poured out without mixture." That is, there shall be no mixture of mercy; there shall be no sort of mitigation or moderation. God sometimes executes judgments upon sinners in this world, but it is with great mixtures of mercy and with restraint. But then there will be full and unmixed wrath.[18]

The last book of the Bible gives the knock-out punch!

> Then I saw a great white throne and him who was seated on it. From his presence earth and sky fled away, and no place was found for them. And I saw the dead, great and small, standing before the throne, and books were opened. Then another book was opened, which is the book of life. And the dead were judged by what was written in the books, according to what they had done. And the sea gave up the dead who were in it, Death and Hades gave up the dead who were in them, and they were judged, each one of them, according to what they had done. Then Death and Hades were thrown into the lake of fire. This is the second death, the lake of fire. And if anyone's name was not found written in the book of life, he was thrown into the lake of fire. (Revelation 20:11-15)

Hell is real! The wrath of God is real! Judgment is real! Through his Word, God graciously has given us a plethora of descriptions of hell, judgment to come upon those who do not believe, and a hint of the magnitude of eternal punishment given to unrepentant sinners. I don't know about you, but I couldn't imagine this for my worst enemy! How much more so, if *you* or one of your loved ones was headed to this eternal banishment of torment.

I would like to leave this section on hell with the following letter written by Jonathan Edwards to his daughter, dated May 27, 1755:

---

18   Strachan and Allen, *Jonathan Edwards on Heaven and Hell*, 2010.

Dear Child,

Though you are a great way off from us, yet you are not of our minds: I am full of concern for you, often think of you, and often pray for you. Though you are at so great a distance from us, and from all your relations, yet this is a comfort to us, that the same God that is here, is also at Onohquaga; and that though you are out of our sight and out of our reach, you are always in God's hands, who is infinitely gracious; and we can go to him, and commit you to his care and mercy. Take heed that you don't forget or neglect him. Always, set God before your eyes, and live in his fear, and seek him every day with all diligence: for 'tis he, and he only can make you happy or miserable, as he pleases; and your life and health, and the eternal salvation of your soul, and your all in this life and that which is to come, depends on his will and pleasure.

This week before last, on Thursday, David died; whom you knew and used to play with, and who used to live at our house. His soul is gone into the eternal world. Whether he was prepared for death we do not know. This is a loud call of God to you to prepare for death. You see that they that are young die, as well as those that are old: David was not very much older than you. Remember what Christ has said, that you must be born again, or you never can see the kingdom of God. Never give yourself any rest, unless you have good evidence that you are converted and become a new creature. We hope that God will preserve your life and health and return you to Stockbridge again in safety; but always remember that your life is uncertain: you know not how soon you must die, and therefore had need to be always ready.

(I have not included the final salutation of this letter).

I am, Your tender and affectionate father, Jonathan Edwards[19]

---

19   Strachan and Allen, *Jonathan Edwards on Heaven and Hell*, 2010.

CHAPTER 7

Eternity in Heaven

T hink of the most beautiful place you have ever been, your Paradise; or think about the most beautiful experience of your life. At the time, you may have thought, *Nothing can top this!* Perhaps you wanted it to last forever. Well, as you know, it didn't last forever. Now, imagine the most spectacular, granddaddy place of them all—heaven. And imagine it lasting forever!

For a true believer, there is nothing that brings more peace, hope, and joy to our souls than knowing that when we die, we will be immediately present with the Lord in heaven for eternity. So too for our loved ones who are believers. Death is not a tragedy for a believer! One moment we are in our bodies; the next; we are in the presence of Jesus. Just listen to Jesus' words to the thief on the cross:

> *One of the criminals who were hanged railed at him, saying, "Are you not the Christ? Save yourself and us!" But the other rebuked him, saying, "Do you not fear God, since you are under the same sentence of condemnation? And we indeed justly, for we are receiving the due reward of our deeds; but this man has done nothing wrong." And he said, "Jesus, remember me when you come into your kingdom." And he said to him, "Truly, I say to you, **today** you will be with me in paradise." (Luke 23:39-43)*

Notice what Jesus said . . . *today*. Not tomorrow or next week or in a month. . . *today*. All too often believers fear death as an end and are saddened by the loss of a loved one. But, think about it. Is this not the most selfish, self-centered viewpoint a person can have as a believer? Ask yourself: Would you really want to have your loved one back, knowing he or she was in the presence of the Lord Jesus? Do we hurt when a loved one dies? Are we in pain, knowing we will miss our loved one? Yes! But let your mourning turn to joy and celebrate the hope that is within you!

I want to reiterate something terribly important. Jesus spoke often about heaven. He referred to heaven as the dwelling place of God. However, my friends, as much as He spoke about heaven, He spoke more about **how to get into heaven!**

The Bible is *the* reference to use when learning about heaven; it is God's revelation to us. It starts in the beginning (Genesis 1:1) when God created heaven and earth, and it concludes at the end of time when God reveals a new heaven and earth (Revelation 21). It is not possible in the space of this book to include every scripture pertaining to heaven. That's not our purpose. However, I do want to share with you scripture references that affirm heaven as a real place, as the dwelling place of God. Additionally, we will look at scripture that describes life in heaven, and how we will recognize and know all the redeemed saints.

The book of Revelation gives us the most descriptive account of the new heaven and earth to come and what it will be like. I have deferred to a commentary on heaven from Jonathan Edwards' sermons on heaven, as well as excerpts from theologians, teachers, and pastors. I pray their insights will bring hope and joy to you, especially during the times of pain and suffering.

Yes! Heaven is a real place! Just like the city, state, or country you live in now. Look what Jesus said to his disciples the night before he was crucified.

> *Let not your hearts be troubled. Believe in God; believe also in me. In my Father's house are many rooms. If it were not so, would I have told you that I go to prepare a place for you? And if I go and prepare a place for you, I will come again and will take you*

to myself, that where I am you may be also. And you know the way to where I am going. Thomas said to him, "Lord, we do not know where you are going. How can we know the way?" Jesus said to him, "I am the way, and the truth, and the life. No one comes to the Father except through me." (John 14:1-6)

In addition to confirming that heaven is a real place, Jesus also told his disciples that it was His dwelling place. And during his earthly ministry, Jesus often referred to God, His Father, as dwelling in heaven. Let's look at a few of these verses where he is describing a real place and God's dwelling:

Jesus said, "I tell you, many will come from east and west and recline at table with Abraham, Isaac, and Jacob in the kingdom of heaven," (Matthew 8:11)

And call no man your father on earth, for you have one Father, who is in heaven. (Matthew 23:9)

For he was looking forward to the city that has foundations, whose designer and builder is God. (Hebrews 11:10)

The LORD *looks down from heaven; he sees all the children of man.* (Psalm 33:13)

Yes, we are of good courage, and we would rather be away from the body and at home with the Lord. (2 Corinthians 5:8)

In his sermon, "Many Mansions," Jonathan Edwards stated: "Heaven is the house where God dwells with his family. Heaven is the place that God has built for himself and his children."[20] *So then you are no longer strangers and aliens, but you are fellow citizens with the saints and members of the* **household of God**. (Ephesians 2:19)

---

20   Jonathan Edwards, *Sermon on Many Mansions*, Dec. 1737.

What Will Heaven Be Like?

In heaven we will experience unending joy and pleasures forevermore. Sorrow and sadness will be gone. Death and tears will be wiped away. We will live in the presence of God, sinless and perfectly righteous before Him. We will spend eternity with angels, every Old Testament saint, New Testament saint, and everyone who has been called home thereafter in perfect communion, knowing each other intimately. There will be no tension, no strife, no competition, no jealousy, no envy, no relationship battles—nothing but perfect love, fellowship, and harmony. Everything we do will be perfect and in perfect harmony with God. Nothing will impair our love, worship, and service to Him. Imagine everlasting joy and gladness. As Isaiah wrote: *And the ransomed of the Lord shall return and come to Zion with singing; everlasting joy shall be upon their heads; they shall obtain gladness and joy, and sorrow and sighing shall flee away.* (Isaiah 35:10)

The last chapter of Revelation sums it up so beautifully:

> *No longer will there be anything accursed, but the throne of God and of the Lamb will be in it, and his servants will worship him. They will see his face, and his name will be on their foreheads. And night will be no more. They will need no light of lamp or sun, for the Lord God will be their light, and they will reign forever and ever.* (Revelation 22:3-5)

Listen to how Dr. MacArthur summarizes heaven in responding to the question, "What Will Heaven Be Like?"

In heaven there will be no sin, suffering, sorrow, or pain. We will never do anything to displease God. There will be no persecution, division, disunity, or hate. In heaven there will be no quarrels or disagreements. There will be no disappointments. There will be no weeping because there will be nothing to make us sad. No more unkind deeds or sinful thoughts. We will be completely and perfectly free from being held hostage to sin and finally able to do that which is absolutely righteous, holy, and perfect before God.[21]

We will become Christ-like, perfect in body and soul. The Apostle John wrote in 1John 3:2: *Beloved, we are God's children now, and what we will be has not yet appeared; but we know that when he appears we shall be like him, because we shall see him as he is.*

Paul tells us in 2 Corinthians 5:1: *For we know that if the tent* (body) *that is our earthly home is destroyed, we have a building from God, a house* (body) *not made with hands, eternal in the heavens.*

Knowing Each Other In Heaven

Will we know each other in heaven? Yes! We will most definitely know each other and intimately. An example of this is found in the story of the transfiguration as recorded in Luke 9:28-36.

Just prior to beginning his last journey to Jerusalem, Jesus went up to a mountain to pray and brought with Him, Peter, James, and John. While He was praying, His countenance (the appearance of His face) altered and His clothes became dazzling white. There were two men talking with Him, Moses and Elijah whom the disciples recognized (although they had never seen them before). Peter then offered to make a tent for the three of them. For Peter, James, and John to know that it was Moses and Elijah with Jesus, gives clear indication that we will recognize saints we have never seen before.

We will also see and know our loved ones. King David expected to see his infant son who had died: *"I shall go to him, but he shall not return to me.* (2 Samuel 12:23) For this to happen, we must maintain our individual identities.

---

21   John MacArthur, *What Will Heaven Be Like?* May 7, 2019.

Let's explore even further. Upon His resurrection, Jesus appeared to many and they knew Him. The Apostle Paul in 1 Corinthians 15:5-8 states: *He appeared to Cephas, then to the twelve. Then he appeared to more than five hundred brothers at one time, most of whom are still alive, though some have fallen asleep. Then he appeared to James, then to all the apostles. Last of all, as to one untimely born, he appeared also to me.* And in the book of Acts:

He presented himself alive to them after his suffering by many proofs, appearing to them during forty days and speaking about the kingdom of God. (1:3)

God gives us enough insight through the Word to know that we will not only be reunited with our families, friends, and loved ones, but we will recognize the saints of all ages. We will have the opportunity in the immeasurable perfection of Heaven to know all the saints of the ages and to grow these relationships. Imagine knowing and having everlasting opportunity with Abraham, Moses, and the Apostles!

In his sermon, "Heaven and Hell," dated Sept. 4, 1855, Charles Spurgeon, using Matthew 8:11-12 as his reference, created a beautiful picture for his congregation about seeing our loved ones and knowing all the other redeemed saints:

> Some people think that in heaven we shall know nobody. But our text declares here, that we "shall sit down with Abraham, and Isaac, and Jacob." Then I am sure that we shall be aware that they are Abraham, and Isaac, and Jacob. I have heard of a good woman, who asked her husband when she was dying, "My dear, do you think you will know me when you and I get to heaven?" "Shall I know you?" he said, "why, I have always known you while I have been here, and do you think I shall be a greater fool when I get to heaven?" I think it was a very good answer. If we have known one another here, we shall know one another there. I have dear departed friends up there, and it is always a sweet thought to me, that when I shall put my foot,

as I hope I may, upon the threshold of heaven, there will come my sisters and brothers to clasp me by the hand and say, "Yes, thou loved one, and thou art here." Dear relatives that have been separated; you will meet again in heaven. One of you has lost a mother—she is gone above; and if you follow the track of Jesus, you shall meet her there. Methinks I see yet another coming to meet you at the door of Paradise; and though the ties of natural affection may be in a measure forgotten,—I may be allowed to use a figure—how blessed would she be as she turned to God, and said, "Here am I, and the children that thou hast given me." We shall recognize our friends—Husband, you will know your wife again. Mother, you will know those dear babes of yours—you marked their features when they lie panting and gasping for breath. You know how ye hung over their graves when the cold sod was sprinkled over them, and it was said, "Earth to earth. Dust to dust, and ashes to ashes." But ye shall hear those loved voices again: ye shall hear those sweet voices once more; ye shall yet know that those whom ye loved have been loved by God. Would not that be a dreary heaven for us to inhabit, where we should be alike unknowing and unknown? I would not care to go to such a heaven as that. I believe that heaven is a fellowship of the saints, and that we shall know one another there. I have often thought I should love to see Isaiah; and, as soon as I get to heaven, methinks, I would ask for him, because he spoke more of Jesus Christ than all the rest. I am sure I should want to find out good George Whitefield—he who so continually preached to the people, and wore himself out with a more than seraphic zeal. O yes! We shall have choice company in heaven when we get there. There will be no distinction of learned and unlearned, clergy and laity, but we shall walk freely one among another; we shall feel that we are brethren; we shall "sit down with Abraham, and Isaac, and Jacob.[22]

---

22   Charles Spurgeon, *Sermon on Heaven and Hell*, Sept. 4, 1855.

What more could be said about how wonderful it will be to spend eternity in the presence of our Creator, saints from old and new, family and friends. No sin, no darkness, no despair, no sadness, no tears only continuous happiness and joy forever! There shouldn't be anything in this sin-cursed world we have today that would be worth holding onto that could mean more than eternity in heaven.

You have now, I am sure, visualized as you read what heaven and hell will be like. Heaven is eternal, hell is eternal, our souls are eternal (and someday our bodies). No one will ever cease to exist, all who have lived in the created world will live forever. Why? Because God is eternal. He is the Creator and He created all that has been created for eternity according to the council of His will (Ephesians 1:11). So, upon the moment of your physical death, your eternal soul will either enter heaven and spend eternity with God, or your eternal soul will enter hell and spend eternity in torment, separated from God.

CHAPTER 8

WHY?

Count it all joy, my brothers, when you meet trials of various kinds,
for you know that the testing of your faith produces steadfastness.
And let steadfastness have its full effect, that you may be perfect
and complete, lacking in nothing. (James 1:1-4)

The Purpose of Suffering, Trials, and Tragedy

For many believers, this section is often misunderstood. To get answers we must turn to James, chapter 1. For believers, going through life's trials is almost certainly anticipated. Understanding and handling them in the right perspective is what keeps us moving forward, bringing us a reassurance of our salvation. However, when tragedy strikes—especially suddenly—it can cause even the most devout follower to question— "Why? Why me? Why us? Why did God allow this to happen?" This is not to say there is any question of trusting God or having a lack of understanding of His sovereignty. Our tragedy affirms Romans 8:28, *And we know that for those who love God all things work together for good, for those who are called according to his purpose.* What I love about this promise is that God is working good in me in the midst of my suffering according to His purpose, His plan.

NOTE—For me personally, this was not a question I ever asked or harbored in my heart. The reason for this was two-fold: First, God poured out his love, peace, and mercy on me immediately; and Second, I had read and understood the book of Job. So, asking why was a moot point for me.

What I found myself asking was, "What is the purpose of it all?" And, "How was God working this out for my good?"

Why Did This Happen to Us?

This is a question every parent, sibling, grandparent, aunt, uncle, cousin, and friend asks when something bad happens, especially over the tragic loss of a loved one. It is a difficult question to address and often goes unanswered. I mean, do any of us really know why they were murdered; why they died of a disease; why they died accidentally; why they committed suicide?

Do we ever really know why? I propose we do not; but God does. I am brought back to the words I spoke at my son's funeral.

> Who are we. . . who am I to question the Great, I AM? God gives and God takes away. Remember, God gave His only son, so that if I (we) believe in Him, have the promise of eternal life; and I (we) would have the opportunity to see Ryan again. Ryan believed this with his whole heart. Asking God, "Why?" will not bring Ryan back, nor will any of us get the answer to why this happened. But knowing I will see him again is a peace, hope, and healing only God can give.

When God calls, there is no need to ask, "Why?" as there is nothing in my humanness that could ever comprehend the answer. So I choose instead to grasp the words of the Lord that are embedded in the deepest, darkest pit of despair: He is with me. This assurance gives victory over death, eternal life over earthly life. It is the promise God gives to those who believe in Him. (John 3:16)

I can think of no man who deserved a better explanation of, "Why?" than Job. Here is a man—a righteous man, mind you—who loved God whole heartedly. In the first chapter of Job, we not only learn that he loves and fears God, is blameless before Him and turns from evil, but that he was also extremely wealthy, had numerous children, cattle, servants, and land. He was identified as one of the greatest men in the East. So, the devil, having a conversation with God, says to Him that the only reason Job was blameless before God was because God had blessed him with all of the pleasures of life and an abundant family, and that if all that was taken from him, he would curse God. So, God allowed the devil to test his theory. He told him (the devil) that he could take everything from Job—his children (his wife was spared), his possessions, his land and cattle, but he could not touch Job. Well, the devil did just that. He wiped Job out completely. All of Job's children were killed when a building collapsed; all his cattle, donkeys, and oxen were stolen; and his servants killed.

Here was Job's response upon hearing of each tragic event:

> *Then Job arose and tore his robe and shaved his head and fell on the ground and worshiped. And he said, "Naked I came from my mother's womb, and naked shall I return. The LORD GAVE, AND THE LORD HAS TAKEN AWAY; BLESSED BE THE NAME OF THE LORD." IN ALL THIS JOB DID NOT SIN OR CHARGE GOD WITH WRONG.* (Job 1:20-22)

Well, just when you think, "Wow! God proved His point to the devil!" It still wasn't enough for the devil. So this time, he told God that Job would surely curse Him if his bone and flesh were afflicted. So, God allowed the devil to inflict Job's body, with the restriction that he could not take his life. So the devil covered Job with loathsome sores from the crown of his head to the soles of his feet, so that Job had to use broken pottery to scrape his skin. This time, his wife had had enough. She begged Job to curse God and die.

To which Job responded:

> *"You speak as one of the foolish women would speak. Shall we receive good from God, and shall we not receive evil?" In all this Job did not sin with his lips.* (Job 2:10)

You may be thinking, "Okay. . . so, this is an ancient biblical story that happened to some other guy. How does it apply to me and my loved ones?" Well, for it to be in God's inspired, infallible Word, means that through the story of Job, God is revealing His sovereignty to us, the answer to suffering and the answer to our, "Why?" While most of us have heard the story of Job, how many have ever read the book of Job or studied it? If you have, then you know God never explains to Job why these things happened to him. We as readers know about the devil's accusation in the heavenly council, but Job does not. And the lesson he learns thirty-eight chapters later has nothing to do with his wanting to understand why. What he learns is God's sovereign control over everything—every being and all that goes on the Earth and in the Universe—as He is the Creator of it all.

A Side Note: Did you notice that the devil could do nothing without the sovereign, providential will of God allowing him to do it? Only God is sovereign. The devil **is not** and can do nothing outside the providential will of God.

There are most likely a wide range of purposes behind the trials, trage-dies, and sufferings in a believer's life. So I am just going to focus on three that have had the greatest impact on me through this experience and many others throughout my lifetime.

Testing of Our Faith

Commitment

God tests our hearts toward Him, as He did with Abraham, Job, and other patriarchs in the Bible. It is His call to use whatever means he deems necessary to bring us to a point of commitment to Him. And to be clear, God doesn't test us to find out the commitment of our heart. He already knows it. His tests are for us, so we can know where we stand with Him. Are we strong in difficult times, knowing He is in complete control, or do we crumble and curse Him because of what we are suffering? Do we persevere, trusting and believing that He is working all things together for good and for His purpose, or are we filled with anxiety, lost, confused, angry, and bitter?

> *In this you rejoice, though now for a little while, if necessary, you have been grieved by various trials, so that the tested genuineness of your faith—more precious than gold that perishes though it is tested by fire—may be found to result in praise and glory and honor at the revelation of Jesus Christ.* (1 Peter 1:6-7)

Idols

Next, we need to evaluate our love for God. In our busy lives, we often place God at the bottom of our priority list. Take a look at the first commandment. The first commandment states: *You shall have no other gods before me.* (Exodus 20:3) Now you might be saying, "Okay. . . I don't serve any other gods. So, what do you mean by idols?" An idol is anything you love, fear, or serve other than God. Do you put more into your children than you do God? Do you put more into your spouse than God? Do you put more into your job, your career, your hobby, or your friends than God? Is music, entertainment, sports, social media, or politics more important to you than God? In our world today, these are our idols, our other gods.

We are all guilty of doing this. John Wesley, in his explanatory notes, sums it up: "Whatever is loved, feared, delighted in, or depended on, more than God, that we make a god of." My friends, is there anything or anyone more important or dearer to you than God? If so, then He is going to remove it. Let's look at two scripture verses, one from the Old Testament and the other from the words of Jesus:

> *If a prophet or a dreamer of dreams arises among you and gives you a sign or a wonder, and the sign or wonder that he tells you comes to pass, and if he says, "Let us go after other gods," which*

you have not known, "and let us serve them," you shall not listen to the words of that prophet or that dreamer of dreams. For the LORD YOUR GOD IS TESTING YOU, TO KNOW WHETHER YOU LOVE THE LORD YOUR GOD WITH ALL YOUR HEART AND WITH ALL YOUR SOUL. (Deuteronomy13:1-3)

Do you see where God specifically states that He is *testing you?*

Another example is the story of Abraham and Isaac in Genesis 22. As you may recall, in Genesis 17, Abraham was given a promise from God that through his seed he would become the father of many nations. At the time, Abraham and Sarah, his wife, were old and childless. Nonetheless, nothing is impossible with God and, low and behold, as promised, Sarah gave birth to Isaac. Fast-forward to Genesis 22: *After these things God tested Abraham and said to him, "Abraham!" And he said, "Here I am." He said, "Take your son, your only son Isaac, whom you love, and go to the land of Moriah, and offer him there as a burnt offering on one of the mountains of which I shall tell you* (verses 1-2). Notice, the text says, *God tested Abraham.* So Abraham does what God has instructed. Jumping to verses 9 and 10: *"When they came to the place of which God had told him, Abraham built the altar there and laid the wood in order and bound Isaac his son and laid him on the altar, on top of the wood. Then Abraham reached out his hand and took the knife to slaughter his son."*

Okay. I don't know about you, but can you imagine God telling you to offer your son, your only son, as a sacrifice to Him? I can only imagine what may have been going on in the mind of Abraham (especially in light of the fact of the promise God had given him earlier), when God told him to sacrifice his son by his own hand! How many of us could do what God told Abraham to do? Verses 11-13: *But the angel of the* LORD *CALLED TO HIM FROM HEAVEN AND SAID, "ABRAHAM, ABRAHAM!" AND HE SAID, "HERE I AM." He said, "Do not lay your hand on the boy or do anything to him, for now I know that you fear God, seeing you have not withheld your son, your only son, from me." And Abraham lifted up his eyes and looked, and behold, behind him was a ram, caught in a thicket by his horns. And Abraham went and took the ram and offered it up as a burnt offering instead of his son.* Because of Abraham's faith in God and His promises, he was willing to let go and give Isaac up because of his love and fear (respect) of God. To conclude, verses 15-18: *And the angel of the* LORD *called to Abraham a second time from heaven and said, "By myself I have sworn, declares the* LORD, *because you have done this and have not withheld your son, your only son, I will surely bless you, and I will surely multiply your offspring as the stars of heaven and as the sand that is on the seashore. And your offspring shall possess the gate of his enemies, and in your offspring shall all the nations of the earth be blessed, because you have obeyed my voice."*

Now that is the trial of all trials! What it shows us is an example of unconditional faith, trust, and commitment to the Lord, that not even a child, an only child, was going to be more important to Abraham than God. This trial was not for God to see what Abraham would do, as He already knew what Abraham would do, but it was for Abraham's benefit, as he proved to himself his unwavering faith and utter trust in God.

Moving to the words of Jesus: *Whoever does not bear his own cross and come after me cannot be my disciple.* (Luke 14:27) Jesus was very clear when He spoke of taking up your cross and following Him. We must be willing to forsake everything we have to be a true disciple. For me, I must ask myself: "Do I love Jesus more than my life, my husband, my children, my losses, my suffering, and even the most precious gift God can give a mother, my son's life?"

Ministering, Mentoring and Helping Others

Lastly, the purpose of our trials and tragedies in life give us the opportunity to minister, mentor, and help others in need. God tells us to, "bear one another's burdens." (Galatians 6:2) A couple of years after Ryan passed, I began serving as a grief mentor. This opportunity led to my desire to become a counselor through the Association of Certified Biblical Counselors (ACBC). God uses this counseling ministry to bring many hurting souls back to the Word to guide them through their trials and tragedies.

In addition to helping others, family and friends of my husband started The Ryan Thomas Foundation. The organization promotes water safety and gives donations to various organizations, such as the Arizona Game and Fish (life vests), and the Drowning Coalition and Outdoor Experience. The Outdoor Experience organization provides a variety of activities for terminally ill children.

God does not spare us from hardship. Suffering, trials, and tragedy will happen to all of us. And, as stated in the introduction, God is no respecter of persons. Under His sovereign control, He not only allows hardships, He plans them, ordains them, permits them, and has a purpose for them. How we get through them depends on the status of our heart. We must have faith that God's grace is sufficient for us and will provide all we need to endure the hardship. Look at these beautiful scriptures of His promises to us when we are going through stormy waters:

> *When you pass through the waters, I will be with you; and through the rivers, they shall not overwhelm you; when you walk through fire you shall not be burned, and the flame shall not consume you.* (Isaiah 43:2)

> *Many are the afflictions of the righteous, but the LORD DELIVERS HIM OUT OF THEM ALL.* (Psalm 34:19)

> *Blessed be the God and Father of our Lord Jesus Christ, the Father of mercies and God of all comfort, who comforts us in all our affliction, so that we may be able to comfort those who are in any*

affliction, with the comfort with which we ourselves are comforted by God. (2 Corinthians 1:3-4)

Here is a promise from our Lord once the storm has passed:

Blessed is the man who remains steadfast under trial, for when he has stood the test, he will receive the crown of life, which God has promised to those who love him. (James 1:12)

Before closing this chapter on the purpose of suffering, we must never forget what Christ did for us. Because without Him, we are all without hope! Jesus Christ—God, the second person of the Trinity; ordained before the foundation of the world, according to the counsel of His will—became incarnate and entered humanity, became a man with two natures, both fully divine and fully human, sacrificed his life (He who was without sin) for the sins of all, a sacrifice God had ordained before the foundation of the world, from eternity past, present, and future. Jesus bore it all, so that we have now been reconciled to God. We have been declared righteous through the blood of Jesus Christ, and with His resurrection He conquered death and remains alive forever and ever. We. too, will have the same! (1 Corinthians 15)

Because of the love of God, His grace and mercy, I have, by no account of my own, the assurance of spending eternal life in heaven with God the Father, Jesus Christ, and the Holy Spirit. And I get to spend eternity with Ryan, all my loved ones, and all who have put their belief, faith, trust, and hope in Jesus Christ alone for their salvation.

These gentle reminders from the Lord, were His way of getting me out of myself and into what not only what He has done for me, but also to pray for those who do not know this kind of hope and peace, and the sufferings others are going through. I have often said that I do not know how any parent gets through the loss of a child without God. To have no hope, no peace, and to continue through life with no understanding, must be one of the most miserable existences ever to endure.

CHAPTER 9

What is Life's Greatest Question?

Most of us, until we are on our death bed or attending to a loved one who is dying, don't think about the afterlife. Why would we? After all, death can be pretty scary, and the subject brings up unwanted emotions, discomfort, and vulnerability. Believe it or not, this question is asked and answered by the Lord Jesus Christ in the parable (a story that teaches a moral or spiritual lesson) of the Good Samaritan. I will specifically reference Luke 10:25. But first, a little background.

Throughout Jesus' ministry, He was often challenged by the Scribes and Pharisees, Jewish religious leaders. The Scribes (also known as lawyers) served as secretaries of the Mosaic law. Their business was to pen the law and prepare and issue decrees. The Pharisees (their name means separated one) were a religious group who often clashed with Jesus over His interpretation of the law. They portrayed themselves as self-righteous, spiritual, students of the law set apart from the common people who did not know or study the law. Both the Scribes and Pharisees were religious hypocrites that Jesus admonished harshly in Matthew 23:1-39.

During one of Jesus' teachings, a noted scribe asked the most important question that could ever be asked: "Teacher, what shall I do to inherit eternal life?" You might be wondering why he asked this question and why it is the greatest question ever asked. Let's explore.

As a nation, the Jewish people were well taught and trained in the Mosaic law, as they were the ones chosen to receive the law of God through Moses. Additionally, the Old Testament scriptures—the writings of the major and minor prophets, psalms, and Job—taught God's promise of an eternal kingdom. This was very much the core of Jewish theology which was passed down from generation to generation. During the time of Jesus' ministry, the Jewish people were well-schooled on the topics of a coming Messiah, a coming eternal Kingdom, and the belief that physical death was not the end of life.

In his book, *Hard Sayings of the Bible*, Walter Kaiser writes, "For the believer in Yahweh (God) in Old Testament times, death did not end it all. There was life after death, and that life was to be in the presence of the living God."[23]

The reason this is the most important question ever asked is that every human soul is immortal, meaning that every human being will live eternally. Our physical shell of a body will die, but **you** will go on as **you** forever. The Jewish nation knew this; hence, perhaps one of the reasons why the scribe asked the question of Jesus.

However, this is not the point, because the lawyer was asking **how** does he inherit eternal life with God. You see, all of us are faced with the question of where and under what condition are we spending eternity.

Looking at Luke 10:25-39, let's find out how Jesus responded to the lawyer:

> *And behold, a lawyer stood up to put him to the test, saying, "Teacher, what shall I do to inherit eternal life?" He said to him, "What is written in the Law? How do you read it?" And he answered, "You shall love the Lord your God with all your heart and with all your soul and with all your strength and with all your mind, and your neighbor as yourself." And he said to him, "You have answered correctly; do this, and you will live."*

---

23   Walter Kaiser, *Hard Sayings of the Bible*, 1996.

But he, desiring to justify himself, said to Jesus, "And who is my neighbor?" Jesus replied, "A man was going down from Jerusalem to Jericho, and he fell among robbers, who stripped him and beat him and departed, leaving him half dead. Now by chance a priest was going down that road, and when he saw him he passed by on the other side. So likewise a Levite, when he came to the place and saw him, passed by on the other side. But a Samaritan, as he journeyed, came to where he was, and when he saw him, he had compassion. He went to him and bound up his wounds, pouring on oil and wine. Then he set him on his own animal and brought him to an inn and took care of him. And the next day he took out two denarii and gave them to the innkeeper, saying, 'Take care of him, and whatever more you spend, I will repay you when I come back.' Which of these three, do you think, proved to be a neighbor to the man who fell among the robbers?" He said, "The one who showed him mercy." And Jesus said to him, "You go, and do likewise."

I don't know about you, but I can tell you that I have failed miserably time and time again with Jesus' response, "You shall love the Lord your God with all your heart, and with all your soul and with all your strength and with all your mind, and your neighbor as yourself." And oh, so much more with Jesus' description of a neighbor. You see friends, these two commandments are a summary of the Mosaic law—the Ten Commandments. Deuteronomy 6:4-5 was the summation of God's law. So, if eternal life requires a perfect love of God and loving our neighbors like we love ourselves, then every human being is guilty, unrighteous, and deserves death. As the Apostle Paul states in Romans 3:10-12: *As it is written, "None is righteous, no, not one; no one understands; no one seeks for God. All have turned aside; together they have become worthless; no one does good, not even one."*

Since we are all born sinners and have fallen short of the glory of God, our only hope lies in the one who is perfect, Jesus Christ. Despite what

 67

every other religion teaches, biblical Christianity is the only religion that is not <u>works-based</u>. You cannot get into heaven based on anything you do on earth. You cannot get to heaven because you go to church every Sunday, tithe, serve, or volunteer. You cannot get to heaven because of any contribution you made while you were on earth. You cannot get into heaven because you were raised in the church or dedicated your life and followed all the rules of a specific religion. You cannot get into heaven because your mother, father, sibling, child, or grandparent is going to heaven. Every soul is on their own. As Ezekiel 18:20 so clearly states: *The soul who sins shall die. The son shall not suffer for the iniquity of the father, nor the father suffer for the iniquity of the son. The righteousness of the righteous shall be upon himself, and the wickedness of the wicked shall be upon himself.* No one will enter heaven without God's specific consent. Let's take a look at God's requirement for entry into heaven and what Jesus did.

Hope = Salvation

God the Son, Jesus, the second person of the Trinity, came down from heaven and was born incarnate of a virgin; being both fully human and fully divine, he lived a sinless life, went to the cross, and became the living sacrifice by taking on all the sins for all whom God had given Him from before the foundation of the world, from eternity past to eternity future, enduring the most humiliating, wretched death that culminated in rejection and brief separation from God His Father (as God cannot look upon sin). Jesus' blood, as it drained from His body, taking every sin for every believer from eternity past to eternity future, washed it whiter than snow. When He uttered the words, "It is finished," He gave us *spiritual* life. By conquering *physical* death through His resurrection, He guaranteed our physical bodily resurrection, as well as uniting our bodies with our souls. He who was righteous did it all so that we might be reconciled with God and considered righteous. 2

Corinthians. 5:21: *For our sake he made him to be sin who knew no sin, so that in him we might become the righteousness of God.* What Adam failed to accomplish (catapulting us all into eternal sin and damnation), Jesus obtained for all of us a renewed opportunity to be reconciled to God, if we believe in Him, putting our faith in Him and in Him alone. Because of God's love for His Son, He gave salvation to those whom He chose from before the foundation of the world. God gave us hope through the sacrifice of His son Jesus to redeem us to Himself, according to the counsel of His will.

Jesus, out of His love for His Father, sacrificed Himself. Why? Jesus, himself lets us know in verse 24 of His prayer to the Father in John 17: *Father, I desire that they also, whom you have given me, may be with me where I am, to see my glory that you have given me because you loved me before the foundation of the world.* Jesus wanted all whom the Father had given Him to be with Him and to see His glory whom He shared with God the Father from eternity past, present, and future. Listen to the words of Jesus and his disciples:

> For God so loved the world that he gave his only Son, that whoever believes in him should not perish but have eternal life. (John 3:16)

> Truly, truly, I say to you, whoever hears my word and believes him who sent me has eternal life. He does not come into judgment but has passed from death to life. (John 5:24)

> Jesus said to her, "I am the resurrection and the life. Whoever believes in me, though he die, yet shall he live, and everyone who lives and believes in me shall never die." (John 11:25-26)

> Jesus said to him, "I am the way, and the truth, and the life. No one comes to the Father except through me." (John 14:6)

And there is salvation in no one else, for there is no other name under heaven given among men by which we must be saved." (Apostle Peter—Acts 4:12)

Whoever has the Son has life; whoever does not have the Son of God does not have life. (Apostle John—1 John 5:12)

I know for many of us we may feel that our sins are too great and that God's gift seems so simplistic and gracious. How could He possibly forgive me for all that I have done—past, present, and even yet to come? Well, that's the beauty of the cross! Christ's righteousness washed us white as snow. Look at this passage from Isaiah 1:18: *Though your sins are like scarlet, they shall be as white as snow; though they are red like crimson, they shall become like wool.* Not only that, God remembers our sins no more. Isaiah 43:25: *I, I am he who blots out your transgressions for my own sake, and I will not remember your sins.* Psalms 103:12: *As far as the east is from the west, so far does he remove our transgressions from us.*

I love what Erwin W. Lutzer wrote in his book, *One Minute After You Die:* "The amount of our sin is not a barrier; it is our *unbelief* that cuts us off from God's mercy and pardon."[24]

What is life's greatest question? Answer: ***How do I inherit eternal life with God?***

---

24   Edwin Lutzer, W., *One Minute After You Die*, 2015.

CHAPTER 10

The Answer to Life's Greatest Question

U sing Jesus' prayer to His Father in John 17:3: ***And this is eternal life, that they know you, the only true God, and Jesus Christ whom you have sent.***

My friends, not only is this the answer to life's greatest question, this is the peace that surpasses all understanding in the midst of our severest trials and sufferings; and oh, so much more in a believer's life. Do you know what Jesus is saying here? *Eternal life is not just time as we know it, it is to always have **perfect and complete knowledge of God and Jesus** from eternity past to eternity future.* This is truly the only thing that matters in life—*to know* that when you, your child, your spouse, your sibling(s), your grandparents, other members of your family, your friends die, your soul and their souls will enter eternity in heaven with God and Jesus. I bring you back again to the conversation I had with my son, two weeks prior to God's call.

I had begun making dinner and Ryan was sitting on the couch watching TV. A story on the news came on about someone who had died. As we were talking about the sadness of the story, Ryan suddenly said to me, "Mom, I am not afraid to die. I know God is in control of both life and death and I know where I am going when I die. I know I will be with God." My initial thought was, *WOW! That was profound. And perhaps a bit out of character for a son who, at times, lived his life on the edge.* But as he looked me in the eyes with the utmost sincerity, I responded: "Ryan, to know *you* have that peace and assurance in God for yourself, gives me no greater peace as a parent."

All else is vanity, as the Preacher says in Ecclesiastes. 1:

> *Vanity of vanities, says the Preacher,*
> *vanity of vanities! All is vanity.*
> *What does man gain by all the toil*
> *at which he toils under the sun?*
> *A generation goes, and a generation comes,*
> *but the earth remains forever.*
> *The sun rises, and the sun goes down,*
> *and hastens to the place where it rises.*
> *The wind blows to the south*
> *and goes around to the north;*
> *around and around goes the wind,*
> *and on its circuits the wind returns.*
> *All streams run to the sea,*
> *but the sea is not full;*
> *to the place where the streams flow,*
> *there they flow again.*
> *All things are full of weariness;*
> *a man cannot utter it;*
> *the eye is not satisfied with seeing,*
> *nor the ear filled with hearing.*
> *What has been is what will be,*
> *and what has been done is what will be done,*
> *and there is nothing new under the sun.*
> *Is there a thing of which it is said,*
> *"See, this is new"?*
> *It has been already*
> *in the ages before us.*
> *There is no remembrance of former things,*
> *nor will there be any remembrance*
> *of later things yet to be*
> *among those who come after.*

Looking again at Chapter 3, verse 11 of Ecclesiastes: *He has made every-thing beautiful in its time. Also, he has put eternity into man's heart, yet so that he cannot find out what God has done from the beginning to the end.*

Now take another look at the conclusion of the Preacher's final analysis of the vanity of life here on earth: *I perceived that there is nothing better for them than to be joyful and to do good as long as they live; also that everyone should eat and drink and take pleasure in all his toil—this is God's gift to man.* **I perceived that whatever God does endures forever; nothing can be added to it, nor anything taken from it. God has done it, so that people fear before him. That which is, already has been; that which is to be, already has been; and God seeks what has been driven away.** (Ecclesiastes 3:12-14)

CHAPTER 11

A Peace that Surpasses All Understanding

A Father's Grief - Part 2

The hours, days, weeks, and months all seemed to run together and Kevin was in deep pain. As I stated in an earlier chapter, life becomes surreal, like you are living in a bubble, or having a nightmare that you keep thinking is going to end. You experience disbelief. Human emotions over-whelm. Kevin didn't have peace. He was hurting so much that at various stages his pain turned to anger, over-whelming sadness, suicidal thoughts, and bouts of utter despair. Some of you might be thinking, "Well, isn't this all part of the grieving process?" The answer is, yes. We all have different journeys of grieving the loss of a loved one. However, *peace* is what I am talking about here. The peace that surpasses all understanding.

I often believe that men (though not all men) have a much harder time dealing with loss than women. Why? Because of the way God created them. God created men to be the head of the household. Men work to take care of the family and it's their natural, internal instinct to protect their wives and children at all costs. When the loss of a child or a wife happens, their whole world of control comes crashing down because they can't fix it! They become quite lost, experience guilt, start blaming themselves, stay stuck, and become a victim.

How many times have you heard people say, "No parent should have to bury their child?" And if they do, it's a living nightmare or hell that never seems to subside. Yes, I do agree that it is one of the most painful experiences in life that one may go through; and yes, it would be a nightmare for those who do not know God or understand His sovereignty. But, how sad—and what a waste of a life—to have no hope and nothing but despair, a broken heart, unable to heal, bitterness that grows and never subsides. How does anyone survive in this life with no hope; much more, to bury a child with no hope?

A Mother's Cry – Part 4

The next couple of hours were a blur as the news was getting around to family and friends. When tragedy strikes, time is like space, endless and daunting; no matter how hard you try, you can't take it all in. Then, everything happens much too quickly and you find yourself wishing it could stop so your mind can catch up; but you want it to pass quickly, because your heart hurts so bad you don't think you can live one more moment. Life becomes surreal, like you are living in a bubble or a having nightmare from which you hope you will awake.

As I struggled to think clearly with a tear-stained face and my heart so heavy I thought it was breaking, I began to experience an overwhelming sense of peace. What was happening?

There was a knock at the door. An officer answered it. My son's friend who was with him that day insisted that he speak with me. He was persistent and kept telling the officer that it was important. When the officer finally let him in, the young man sat on the couch and held my hands. He then proceeded to tell me what had happened.

"Ryan told us he had to pee. He jumped into the water and was gone."

At that moment, that exact second, God spoke to me through the Spirit, piercing my broken heart. God said, "He is with me. I took him home." *God had called.*

Peace came over me, because I knew there is no greater victor over physical death than eternal life. Ryan's soul had slipped into the hands of God and heaven became his permanent home.

Just as King David knew he would see his infant son again (2 Samuel 12:23), I knew I would see Ryan again; and as a mother, hope was renewed and comfort restored.

Many have often asked, what do you mean he just jumped in the water and was gone? Did he hit his head? Did he get caught in weeds? Was alcohol a factor? How is it that he just jumped in and was gone, especially if he was such a good swimmer? For me, this is a moot issue, however, I know for many, you may be wondering if there was some other contributing factor. An autopsy was performed to determine cause of death. In the words of the medical examiner who performed the procedure, Ryan's external and internal physical body was "unremarkable." In addition to him being a good swimmer, he had not struck his head, he had not gotten entangled in any weeds, his physique was excellent, with all internal organs healthy. Ryan had been drinking some beer throughout the course the day, however, the medical examiner did not contribute this as a determinant to his final conclusion. The medical examiner's final conclusion reads as follows: *"After considering the known circumstances surrounding the death and the findings on postmortem examination of the body, it is my opinion that Ryan Thomas, a 21-year-old white male, died from drowning. The manner of death "is accident."*

Don't get me wrong, my heart continued to ache. During great trials our human emotions overtake us and God does not take away the pain. Trust me when I say He seems far away and you wonder why, or how He could let something like this happen. But then, He pours out His grace to those He loves and gives us strength to endure the unendurable.

God's promise is that He will never leave us nor forsake us, even in the midst of unimaginable suffering. For me, I can't imagine what it would be like to go through the pain of losing a child, not knowing if I would ever see him again. How could anyone?

As a believer, I can live my life and be excited that when my earthly life is over, I will see Jesus and Ryan and be with them for eternity. All because of God's amazing grace and His promise of salvation. Because of the sacrifice of His son, we can have this hope and peace. Why wouldn't anyone want this? Eternal life. Seeing our loved ones. This is the peace I am talking about.

We are all living on borrowed time. Have you suffered a near death experience? Possibly a heart-attack, or a close call with cancer that is now in remission, or a near fatal car accident? Perhaps your doctor has given you a projected life expectancy, or news of an inoperable tumor? For those who have come close to death and survived, *you* have been given a new chance to get your heart and soul right with God. The fact that you are still alive is because of God's mercy. Don't waste it! You *can be* assured of where you will be spending eternity. You *can be* assured of where your loved ones will spend eternity. You *can have* the peace of knowing that all is well with your soul and the souls of your loved ones.

My friends, death comes to us all. The death of a child is one of the most painful sufferings a parent can endure in their lifetime. And as I have said so many times before, how does one survive such a tragedy without God? The real tragedy is not the loss of a loved one, but the uncertainty of not knowing where your loved one's soul is spending eternity. But even greater than that: If God should require your soul today, where will you spend eternity? How do you know? What assurance do you have?

The Preacher in the last two verses of Ecclesiastes 12:13-14, sums it up with these words: *The end of the matter; all has been heard. Fear God and keep his commandments, for this is the whole duty of man. For God will bring every deed into judgment, with every secret thing, whether good or evil.*

CHAPTER 12

Assurance vs. No Assurance

A few months after Ryan passed, God once again showered his love on me. I had a dream/vision and in my dream/vision, I am watching myself as if my life was a movie. I saw myself lying on my bed asleep. Suddenly, I was frozen and couldn't move my body, as though I was chained to the bed. I was scared and frightened and barely able to breathe. Then, I saw someone (a bodily figure) coming through the window in an incredibly bright light, shining as the sun. As I lay motionless, the being came toward me, and I suddenly found myself crying out, "Ryan? Ryan, is that you?" There was no answer, only the most beautiful, perfect creature I had ever seen. I was kissed on the cheek and encompassed with an indescribable love and peace that penetrated my soul and body. I cried out again, "Ryan? Ryan is that you? You are so beautiful!" (His appearance was similar to the way the Bible describes the angel Gabriel.) Then, he was gone. Again, with no words being spoken.

I woke up and began to cry. All I could do was wonder what had happened and thank God for whatever He revealed to this mother in her deepest pain.

I wanted to believe that it was Ryan who had visited me in my dream, because my loss and emotions were still so raw. However, the Bible is clear that we do not see our loved ones again this side of heaven, despite what Hollywood movies portray. But what the Bible does teach is that angels (Greek for messengers) are sent from God to minister to believers. Hebrews

1:14: Are they not all ministering spirits sent out to serve for the sake of those who are to inherit salvation?

God sent an angel to me through either a vision or a dream simply to kiss me on the cheek and shower me with tremendous love, comfort, and assurance—assurance of His love, and His salvation of eternal life through Jesus Christ. Not only my assurance, but Ryan's as well.

Dr. John Piper states: "Everything angels do, everywhere in the world, at all times, is for the good of Christians. An angel who does something by God's assignment anywhere in the world is fulfilling the promise that God will work all things for the good of all Christians everywhere. This is a sweeping and stunning promise. All angels serve for the good of all Christians, all the time. They are agents of Romans 8:28." [25]

Wow! I did not know this until many years later.

The Apostle John, through the Spirit of God, penned in 1 John, chapter 3 what we need to know to have full assurance of our salvation in Christ and to have the peace of knowing our souls will spend eternity in Heaven. In the following paragraphs is a description of a soul with no assurance and a description of a soul with assurance. Take a moment and read about how you can truly know, if it is well with your soul.

A Soul With No Assurance

Everyone who makes a practice of sinning also practices lawlessness; sin is lawlessness. You know that he appeared in order to take away sins, and in him there is no sin. No one who abides in him keeps

---

25   John Piper, *The Surprising Role of Guardian Angels*, April 4, 2017.

on sinning; no one who keeps on sinning has either seen him or known him. Little children, let no one deceive you. Whoever practices righteousness is righteous, as he is righteous. Whoever makes a practice of sinning is of the devil, for the devil has been sinning from the beginning. The reason the Son of God appeared was to destroy the works of the devil. No one born of God makes a practice of sinning, for God's seed abides in him; and he cannot keep on sinning, because he has been born of God. By this it is evident who are the children of God, and who are the children of the devil: whoever does not practice righteousness is not of God, nor is the one who does not love his brother. (1 John 3:4-8)

The Apostle speaks bluntly in a way all of us can understand. Either we practice the character of God's righteousness by obeying His law, or we practice the sin-filled character of the devil by disregarding the Word and habitually sinning. The key word is practice. God's seed practices righteousness. The devil's seed practices sinning.

A Soul With Assurance

By this we shall know that we are of the truth and reassure our heart before him; for whenever our heart condemns us, God is greater than our heart, and he knows everything. Beloved, if our heart does not condemn us, we have confidence before God; and whatever we ask we receive from him, because we keep his commandments and do what pleases him. And this is his commandment, that we believe in the name of his Son Jesus Christ and love one another, just as he has commanded us. Whoever keeps his commandments abides in God, and God in him. And by this we know that he abides in us, by the Spirit whom he has given us. (1 John 3:19-24)

God is the chief judge and He is far greater than our hearts. Are we convicted by sin? If we are true believers, our hearts will be convicted by truth and sin. But if our hearts do not convict us, then we can be confident in our obedience to God in keeping his commandments and our love for our fellow believers, thus giving us the assurance that the Spirit of God abides in us.

APPENDIX 1

Common Questions and Answers

1. **Do I really believe in the sovereignty of God? If so, to what degree?**

    Most, if not all Christians believe that God is sovereign. However, many don't believe or understand that He is intricately involved in everybody and everything all the time. It is crucial as a believer to have a true, in depth understanding of God's sovereignty. Re-read the Chapter 4, "Understanding the Sovereignty of God". I also recommend *The Sovereignty of God* by A.W. Pink and *The Attributes of God* by Steven Lawson.

2. **Why did God allow this to happen? How could God love me and let me go through this? How could He take my child, my husband, my wife?**

    You may never know why God allowed your suffering or tragedy to take place. But as a believer, Romans 8:28 can provide you with hope and comfort: *And we know that for those who love God all things work together for good, for those who are called according to his purpose.* This verse is a constant, gentle reminder of God's love for us. Ask yourself how you can glorify Him in the midst of your suffering. Read the book of Job. Study it. Job never knew why God did what He did, yet still he choose to trust God. In the end, God's ways are not our ways and God, the Creator, does not owe us, the creature, the answer to our, "Why?"

Everyone suffers and experiences trials in their life. Our sin promises that. So, whether you are a believer or not, God is no respecter of persons. The purpose behind our suffering can be a myriad of reasons. For me, I named three in Chapter 8, "Why?" Take a hard look at yourself. Ask where you are with God, and then ask Him to show you what you need to learn.

3. **Is my loved one in heaven?**

As a biblical counselor, this is probably the most difficult question to address. God is the only one who makes that final determination, as He is the discerner of our hearts. The beauty of our salvation in Jesus Christ is that by God's grace, those who believe through faith in Christ alone will be saved. As Romans 10:9-10 states: *If you confess with your mouth that Jesus is Lord and believe in your heart that God raised him from the dead, you will be saved. For with the heart one believes and is justified, and with the mouth one confesses and is saved.* This is God's promise!

God is perfectly righteous and perfectly just! Genesis 18:25: *Shall not the Judge of all the earth do right.* This verse should bring great comfort to many of us if we are unsure of the destination of our loved one's souls. Not only is God sovereign, He is perfectly righteous and perfectly just, and it is He alone who sees and judges our hearts. It is through His perfect righteousness and justice that all human beings have been offered a way to escape His righteous justice. This is the grace and the trust we all must rest on, as all souls are His.

4. **What is my assurance of heaven?**

In the first of his three letters, the Apostle John gives us the most beautiful assurance in a few short verses: *And this is the testimony, that God gave us eternal life, and this life is in his Son. Whoever has the Son has life; whoever does not have the Son of God does not have life. I write these things to you who believe in the name of the Son of God, that you may know that you have eternal life.* (1 John 5:11-13) Every believer should memorize these verses.

The Apostle Paul emphatically states: *For I am sure that neither death nor life, nor angels nor rulers, nor things present nor things to come, nor powers, nor height nor depth, nor anything else in all creation, will be able to separate us from the love of God in Christ Jesus our Lord. Paul was convinced of this promise and so must we be as well.* (Romans 8:38-39)

The Apostle Paul also teaches us to do a self-inventory: *"Examine yourselves, to see whether you are in the faith. Test yourselves. Or do you not realize this about yourselves, that Jesus Christ is in you? unless indeed you fail to meet the test!* (2 Corinthians 13:5)

There are many people who say they are Christians, believe in Jesus and what He did on the cross and in His resurrection, yet who do not live Christ-honoring lives: *No one born of God makes a practice of sinning, for God's seed abides in him; and he cannot keep on sinning, because he has been born of God.* (1 John 3:9) Does your life bear love for God, repentance of sin, love of your neighbor, obedient living, and a desire to know God through reading and studying the Word? If not, press on my friend, and He will reward your diligence.

5. **Will I see my loved one again?**

Go back and read the chapter on heaven (Chapter 7). King David knew and accepted the consequences of his actions with Bathsheba. When he learned of the death of his infant son, he made the following statement: *But now he is dead. Why should I fast? Can I bring him back again? I shall go to him, but he will not return to me.* (2 Samuel 12:23)

What is wonderful and amazing about this statement is that despite his grievous sin against God, he had assurance that he would see his infant son again. There are two things that formed the foundation of King David's assurance: 1) He confessed and repented; 2) God forgave him.

The question we must ask ourselves is, *"What is my assurance that I will see my loved one in heaven?"*

6. **I'm a believer, why don't I have true peace?**

To help you answer your own question, I would ask you these questions: "Where are you putting your focus? Are you focused on yourself and what you think you are not getting or not feeling? Where are you putting your faith? Your trust? If you are trying to find answers outside of God and His spoken Word, you are not going to find peace. Take a look at what Jesus, who knows our hearts, said to his disciples when they were hurting: *Let not your hearts be troubled. Believe in God; believe also in me. In my Father's house are many rooms. If it were not so, would I have told you that I go to prepare a place for you? And if I go and prepare a place for you, I will come again and will take you to myself, that where I am you may be also.* (John 14:1-3)

First, we must *believe* in Jesus. We must embrace who He is and what He says. Second, know that our sufferings and trials in this life are temporary, as we are only on this earth for a brief time. God is sovereign and has already predestined it all. Just like the Preacher said: *I perceived that whatever God does endures forever; nothing can be added to it, nor anything taken from it. God has done it, so that people fear before him. That which is, already has been; that which is to be, already has been.* (Ecclesiastes 3: 14-15)

7. **I'm stuck and can't move forward, what do I do?**

   Make an appointment to talk with your pastor or elder. Perhaps your church is affiliated with biblical counseling center or has resources to direct you to a biblical counselor.

If You Are an Unbeliever

1. **Why did this happen? Will I ever know why?**

   Everyone suffers and experiences trials in life. Whether you are a believer or not, God is no respecter of persons. The purpose of our suffering can be a myriad of reasons. For me, I named three in the chapter "Why?" (Chapter 8). Take a hard look at yourself and where you are with God. Ask Him to show you what you need to learn.

2. **If there is a God, how could He allow this to happen?**

   I cannot express enough how important it is to know and have a true understanding of the sovereignty of God. God reigns and controls everything and everybody. He is no respecter of persons. Just as good comes, so does evil. When tragedy strikes or suffering takes place, He has allowed it to take place. Why? For His purposes and according to the counsel of His will (Ephesians 1:11). God's ways are not our ways. So often the creature (man), tries to put himself on the same level with the Creator (God). This is impossible.

3. **Is my loved one in heaven?**

   God is righteous and just! Genesis 18:25: *Shall not the Judge of all the earth do right?* What this verse is telling us is that God is our sovereign Judge of righteousness and judgment. He gives grace and mercy to all who call on Him. What none of us knows is the heart – only God knows the heart. Because He is the Creator of Heaven, the Earth and all mankind, and as we have learned that *all souls are*

His, (Ezekiel 18:4), we can and must trust that being the righteous God that He is, we can rest in His justice.

Better question: Ask yourself, "If I were to die today, would I go to heaven?" In 2 Samuel 12:23, King David knew he would see his infant son again. How did he have this assurance? Afterall, he committed adultery. He had his mistress's husband put on the front lines of battle to ensure his death—so add murder to his list of sins. David, a sinner of sinner's like us all, did two things: 1) He repented from the depths of his heart and soul and cried for mercy to be forgiven; 2) He had a true depth of understanding of the depravity of his sin. As he states in Psalm 51:4: *Against you, you only, have I sinned and done what is evil in your sight, so that you may be justified in your words and blameless in your judgment.* David realized that it was God and God alone against whom he had sinned, and that God was absolutely justified in His righteous judgment. God in His grace and mercy forgave David because of his repentant heart.

4. **How can I find peace in the midst of such pain?**
   The only peace you will ever know is when you put your belief, faith, and trust in Jesus Christ alone. You will never find peace through alcohol, drugs, money, sex, or power. None of these superficial remedies can heal a broken heart or remove the guilt of sin.

5. **How do I become a believer in Jesus?**
   Believe - John 11:25: *Jesus said to her, I am the resurrection and the life. Whoever believes in me, though he die, yet shall he live.*

   Confess Christ as your Lord and Savior – Romans 9:9-10: *If you confess with your mouth that Jesus is Lord and believe in your heart that God raised him from the dead, you will be saved. For with the heart one believes and is justified, and with the mouth one confesses and is saved."*

Confess your sins - 1 John 1:9: *If we confess our sins, he is faithful and just to forgive us our sins and to cleanse us from all unrighteousness.*

Love God – Matthew 22:37: *You shall love the Lord your God with all your heart and with all your soul and with all your mind.* John 14:15: *If you love me, you will keep my commandments.*

Love Your Brother – John 13:34: *A new commandment I give to you, that you love one another: just as I have loved you, you also are to love one another. By this all people will know that you are my disciples, if you have love for one another.*

6. **What are my next steps?**
   - Seek out a Bible teaching church. Meet with the pastor or an elder and share that you are a new believer and are looking for guidance on your walk of a Christian life.
   - Get baptized.
   - Get a good Study Bible and begin reading it. (I recommend the *MacArthur Study Bible*–ESV or *The Reformation Study Bible*–ESV.)
   - Begin praying. Just simply start talking to God. He is your friend. Remember, He knows all that is in your heart already, so start sharing and cast all your cares upon Him.

APPENDIX 2

Recommended Resources

MacArthur Study Bible – English Standard Version (ESV)

The Reformation Study Bible – English Standard Version (ESV)

One Minute After You Die - Erwin W. Lutzer

The Gospel According to Jesus - Dr. John MacArthur

Jonathan Edwards on Heaven and Hell - Owen Strachan & Douglas Allen Sweeney

The Attributes of God (Teaching Series) - Dr. Steven Lawson

The Sovereignty of God - Arthur W. Pink

Don't Waste Your Life - John Piper

Trusting God, Even When Life Hurts – Jerry Bridges

APPENDIX 3

Additional Scriptures References

Eternity and Eternal Life
- Psalm 23:6
- Psalm 37:28
- Psalm 56:13
- John 17:2-3
- John 10:27-28
- 1 John 5:11
- John 3:16

Created in the Image of God
- Matthew 10:28
- Matthew 16:26

The Sovereignty of God
- Isaiah 46:9-10
- Psalm 103:19
- Revelation 4:11

The Ways God Is Sovereign
- Psalm 115:3
- Isaiah 14:27
- Isaiah 55:11
- Isaiah 46:9-10

God's Sovereignty Over Nations
- Psalm 103:19
- Proverbs 16:4
- Job 12:23-24

- Isaiah 40:17-18
- Isaiah 40:21-23

God's Sovereignty Over Trials and Suffering

- Daniel 4:35
- James 5:10
- Romans 5:3-4
- John 16:33
- Romans 8:28

God's Sovereignty Over Life and Death

- 1 Samuel 2:6
- James 4:13-16
- Romans 8:28

Eternity in Hell

- Isaiah 53:6
- Matthew 8:12
- Matthew 22:13
- Matthew 25:31-46

Eternity in Heaven

- Matthew 7:11
- Matthew 10:32-33
- Hebrews 11:10
- Philippians 1:21-23

Hope, Salvation, and Peace

- Mark 16:16
- John 3:3-8
- John 3:15-17
- John 3:35-36
- John 8:51
- John 17:1-3
- Ephesians 2:8-9
- 2 Timothy 1:9

Bibliography Sources

Easton's Bible Dictionary and King James Bible, n.d.

Henry, Matthew. *Matthew Henry's Commentary of the Whole Bible – Six Volumes*, 2014,

Hendrickson Publishers.

The ESV® Bible (The Holy Bible, English Standard Version®). ESV® Text Edition: 2016. Copyright © 2001 by Crossway, a publishing ministry of Good News Publishers. The ESV® text has been reproduced in cooperation with and by permission of Good News Publishers.

Kaiser, Walter C. *Hard Sayings of the Bible*. Leicester: Inter Varsity, 1996.

Lawson, Steven. *"How to Be Sure of Your Salvation"*, August 2, 1010.

https://billygraham.org/story/how-to-be-sure-of-your-salvation

Ligonier Ministries, LLC. *The Attributes of God – Teaching Series*, (2014), Steven Lawson, Ligonier.org 800.435.4343.

Lutzer, Erwin, W. *One Minute After You Die*, 2015.

MacArthur Study Bible, English Standard Version (ESV), 2010.

Merriam-Webster Dictionary

"Most Americans Still Believe in God", June 29, 2016. Accessed May 12, 2019, https://news.gallup.com/poll/193271/americans-believe-god.aspx.

Owen Strachan and Douglas Sweeney Allen, *Jonathan Edwards on Heaven and Hell*, 2010.

Pink, Arthur W. *The Attributes of God*. Chapel Library, 1993.

Pink, Arthur W. *The Sovereignty of God*, Chapel Library, 1999.

The Spurgeon Center/heaven-and-hell, Sept. 4, 1855. Accessed May 12, 2019. https://www.spurgeon.org/resource-library/sermons/heavenandhell

Strong, James. *Strong's Exhaustive Concordance to the Bible*, 2009.

"The Surprising Role of Guardian Angels/Desiring God", n.d. Accessed May 12, 2019. https://desiringgod.org/articles/the-surprising-role-of-guardian-angles.

"Wesley's Explanatory Notes Bible Commentary", n.d. Accessed May 12, 2019. https://biblestudy tools.com/commentaries/wesleys-explanatory-notes

"Westminster Confession of Faith", 1647. https://www.ligonier.org/learn/articles/westminster-confession-faith

"What Will Heaven Be Like?", May 7, 2019. https://www.gty.org/library/questions/QA111 COPYRIGHT ©2019 Grace to You

"Will We Recognize and Be Reunited With Our Loved Ones In Heaven?", n.d. https://www.gty.org/library/questions/QA100 COPYRIGHT ©2019 Grace to You

"Why Does Evil Dominate the World?", Mar. 4, 2007. https://www.gty.org/library/sermons-library/90-333

"A Testimony of One Surprised to Be in Hell, Part 1", Apr. 23, 2006. https://www.gty.org/library/sermons-library/42-212/a-testimony-of-one-surprised-to-be-in-hell-part-1